T0336104

Mastering GNOME

Mastering GNOME helps the reader master the GNOME desktop environment for a faster and more robust computing experience.

The best thing about Linux is the plethora of choices that users tend to get. Whether it pertains to the kernel modules, or to the desktop environments, there is no shortage of options.

Speaking of desktop environments, GNOME stands tall as one of the leading options.

GNOME is an open source, free to use, simple, and attractive workspace interface supporting almost all the major Linux operating systems. GNOME includes a beautiful collection of programs, libraries, plugins, and probably millions of themes (some of which you may need to install manually). In fact, one of the most exemplary aspects of GNOME is GNOME Boxes, which allows you to construct virtual networks of multiple Linux operating systems without having to visit the website or download an iOS file, and it runs perfectly well via virtualization on KVM, which is the icing on the cake. But that is not all – GNOME is, inarguably, the single most stable and dependable Linux desktop environment today!

GNOME has become one of the most effective, secure, and trustworthy desktops offered for the Linux platform, and that is the primary reason why it is the desktop environment of choice for Ubuntu, the world's most popular Linux distro.

Regardless of skillset, users can quickly get to speed with GNOME for everyday usage. This is where *Mastering GNOME* comes in.

With *Mastering GNOME*, using GNOME for day-to-day computing becomes a charm, and will help readers undoubtedly boost their productivity.

Mastering Computer Science series is edited by Sufyan bin Uzayr, a writer and educator with over a decade of experience in the computing field.

Mastering Computer Science
Series Editor: Sufyan bin Uzayr

Mastering GNOME: A Beginner's Guide
Jaskiran Kaur, Mathew Rooney, and Reza Nafim

Mastering Flutter: A Beginner's Guide
Divya Sachdeva, NT Ozman, and Reza Nafim

Mastering Vue.js: A Beginner's Guide
Lokesh Pancha, Divya Sachdeva, and Faruq KC

Mastering GoLang: A Beginner's Guide
Divya Sachdeva, D Nikitenko, and Aruqqa Khateib

Mastering KDE: A Beginner's Guide
Jaskiran Kaur, Mathew Rooney, and Shahryar Raz

Mastering Kotlin: A Beginner's Guide
Divya Sachdeva, Faruq KC, and Aruqqa Khateib

For more information about this series, please visit: https://www.routledge
.com/Mastering-Computer-Science/book-series/MCS

The "Mastering Computer Science" series of books are authored by the Zeba Academy team members, led by Sufyan bin Uzayr.

Zeba Academy is an EdTech venture that develops courses and content for learners primarily in STEM fields, and offers education consulting to Universities and Institutions worldwide. For more info, please visit https://zeba.academy

Mastering GNOME
A Beginner's Guide

Edited by
Sufyan bin Uzayr

CRC Press
Taylor & Francis Group
Boca Raton London New York

CRC Press is an imprint of the
Taylor & Francis Group, an **informa** business

First edition published 2023
by CRC Press
6000 Broken Sound Parkway NW, Suite 300, Boca Raton, FL 33487-2742

and by CRC Press
4 Park Square, Milton Park, Abingdon, Oxon, OX14 4RN

CRC Press is an imprint of Taylor & Francis Group, LLC

© 2023 Sufyan bin Uzayr

Library of Congress Cataloging-in-Publication Data

Names: Bin Uzayr, Sufyan, editor.
Title: Mastering GNOME : a beginner's guide / edited by Sufyan bin Uzayr.
Description: First edition. | Boca Raton : CRC Press, 2023. |
Series: Mastering computer science
Identifiers: LCCN 2022020962 (print) | LCCN 2022020963 (ebook) |
ISBN 9781032318998 (hardback) | ISBN 9781032318967 (paperback) |
ISBN 9781003311942 (ebook)
Subjects: LCSH: GNOME (Computer file) | Linux. | Graphical user interfaces
(Computer systems) | Computer software--Development.
Classification: LCC QA76.9.U83 M38156 2023 (print) | LCC QA76.9.U83 (ebook) |
DDC 005.4/37--dc23/eng/20220815
LC record available at https://lccn.loc.gov/2022020962
LC ebook record available at https://lccn.loc.gov/2022020963

ISBN: 9781032318998 (hbk)
ISBN: 9781032318967 (pbk)
ISBN: 9781003311942 (ebk)

DOI: 10.1201/9781003311942

Typeset in Minion
by KnowledgeWorks Global Ltd.

Contents

Preface

The *Mastering Computer Science* series covers a wide range of topics, spanning programming languages as well as modern-day technologies and frameworks. The series has a special focus on beginner-level content, and is presented in an easy-to-understand manner, comprising:

- Crystal-clear text, spanning various topics sorted by relevance,

- A special focus on practical exercises, with numerous code samples and programs,

- A guided approach to programming, with step-by-step tutorials for the absolute beginners,

- Keen emphasis on real-world utility of skills, thereby cutting the redundant and seldom-used concepts and focusing instead on industry-prevalent coding paradigms, and

- A wide range of references and resources to help both beginner and intermediate-level developers gain the most out of the books.

The *Mastering Computer Science* series of books start from the core concepts, and then quickly move on to industry-standard coding practices, to help learners gain efficient and crucial skills in as little time as possible. The books assume no prior knowledge of coding, so even the absolute newbie coders can benefit from this series.

The *Mastering Computer Science* series is edited by Sufyan bin Uzayr, a writer and educator with more than a decade of experience in the computing field.

About the Author

Sufyan bin Uzayr is a writer, coder, and entrepreneur with over a decade of experience in the industry. He has authored several books in the past, pertaining to a diverse range of topics, ranging from History to Computers/IT.

Sufyan is the Director of Parakozm, a multinational IT company specializing in EdTech solutions. He also runs Zeba Academy, an online learning and teaching vertical with a focus on STEM fields.

Sufyan specializes in a wide variety of technologies, such as JavaScript, Dart, WordPress, Drupal, Linux, and Python. He holds multiple degrees, including ones in Management, IT, Literature, and Political Science.

Sufyan is a digital nomad, dividing his time between four countries. He has lived and taught in universities and educational institutions around the globe. Sufyan takes a keen interest in technology, politics, literature, history, and sports, and in his spare time, he enjoys teaching coding and English to young students.

Learn more at sufyanism.com.

CHAPTER 1

Introduction to GNOME

IN THIS CHAPTER

> ➤ Ubuntu-based on GNU/Linux

> ➤ Open Source Linux desktop environment

> ➤ Useful terms (GUI, CLI, TUI)

> ➤ GNOME

> ➤ GNOME-based Linux distributions

> ➤ History of Ubuntu GNOME

> ➤ GNOME 1, GNOME2, GNOME 3

> ➤ Features

> ➤ Advantages and disadvantages

Here in this chapter, we will briefly discuss one of the best flavors of Ubuntu named GNOME. Primarily, it is an official flavor of Ubuntu and features the GNOME desktop environment. Ubuntu flavor GNOME is a mostly pure GNOME desktop experience built from the Ubuntu repositories. Its first (unofficial) release was 12.10 (Quantal Quetzal) in October 2012. The Ubuntu GNOME team announced our first release as an official Ubuntu Derivative: Ubuntu GNOME 13.04. Its first official release was 13.04.

DOI: 10.1201/9781003311942-1

There are various terms to discuss to understand the concept of the Ubuntu GNOME. So let's begin this with Ubuntu and then move forward to the desktop environment GNOME.

Now we are going to cover basic terms before going deep into the GNOME desktop environment such as GNU/Linux, Open Source, Free Software, GUI, TUI, CLI, and so on.

UBUNTU-BASED ON GNU/LINUX

Ubuntu is a "distribution" of GNU/Linux. Linux is the kernel layer. The software talks directly to the hardware: managing power, multitasking, and other low-level functions. Most Linux distributions include the GNU libraries and applications, including development tools, often referred to as GNU/Linux.

What Is Distribution?

The term "distribution" refers to the combination of these packaging of the kernel with the GNU libraries and applications. Ubuntu is one such distribution. It contains the Linux kernel, GNU tools, and many other applications and libraries.

OPEN SOURCE LINUX DESKTOP ENVIRONMENT

The word "Open Source" is the attribute to the Linux community, which brought it into existence along with the introduction of Linux. "Linux" came into existence as only based on kernel.

Many people and communities started contributing toward making it a complete Operating System, which could replace UNIX.

Free Software

"Free software" term is the software that respects users' freedom and community. Approximately, it means that users have the freedom to do anything, such as run, copy, distribute, study, change, and improve the software. Therefore, "free software" is a topic of liberty, not price.

A program is a free software that adequately gives users all of these freedoms. Otherwise, it is nonfree.

Key Points

- The freedom to run the program as per your wish

- Free software can be commercial

- The freedom to get the source code and make changes

- Legal considerations

- Contract-based licenses

Next, we will discuss the following terms, which are also related to the Ubuntu desktop environment GNOME. The useful terms such as GUI, CLI, and TUI are described below.

GUI (Graphical User Interface)

GNOME is the default GUI for most Ubuntu installations and is (loosely) based on the Apple ecosystem.

A GUI or graphical application is anything you can interact with using your mouse, touchpad, or touch screen. You have various icons and other visual prompts that you can activate with a mouse pointer to access the functionalities. DE provides the GUI to interact with your system. For various tasks, you can use GUI applications such as GIMP, VLC, Firefox, LibreOffice, and file manager.

CLI (Command Line Interface)

CLI is a command-line program that accepts inputs to perform a particular function. Any application you can use via commands in the terminal falls into this category.

TUI (Terminal User Interface)

TUI is also known as a Text-based User Interface. You have text on the screen because they are used only in the terminal. These applications are not well-known to many users, but there are a bunch of them. Terminal-based web browsers are an excellent example of TUI programs. Terminal-based games also fall into this category.

WHAT IS GNOME?

GNOME is an open-source movement, part of the GNU project and free software, or it is similar to the Windows desktop system that works on UNIX and UNIX-like systems. It is not dependent on any other window manager. The current version runs on Linux, FreeBSD, IRIX, and Solaris.

"The GNOME project provides two things:

- The GNOME desktop environment, a built-in and attractive desktop for users,

- The GNOME development platform, a comprehensive framework for building applications that integrate into the rest of the desktop."

So, GNOME is the software that helps users and experts to develop a desktop and that can be used for GNU.

Ubuntu GNOME Remix

Ubuntu GNOME is called GNOME Remix. It is a Linux distribution distributed as open-source and free software.

It is used as a GNOME 3 desktop environment with the GNOME Shell instead of the Unity graphical shell. It became a "flavor" of the Ubuntu OS, starting with the 13.04 version was announced in April 2007 that 17.04. Staring with its 17.10 version, the distribution was canceled in the favor of standard Ubuntu, which changed from devoting Unity to GNOME Shell because of its desktop environment.

What Is GNOME GNU?

In 1984, the GNU Project was established to develop a complete UNIX-like operating system with free software, i.e., the GNU system.

GNU kernel is not finished, so GNU is used with Linux. GNU and Linux are combined with the GNU/Linux operating system, now used by millions.

GNU stands for "GNU, Not UNIX." It means that it is an independent system that currently uses Linux kernel and provides an open-source operating system to users.

What Is Ubuntu GNOME in Linux?

Linux is a free UNIX-type operating system initially designed by Linus Torvalds with other developers around the world. It was developed under the GNU, which is General Public License (GPL). The source code for the Linux distro is freely available to everyone over the Internet.

The last GNOME 3 version, which is its latest iteration, is currently one of the most popular desktop environments used by almost every major Linux distro. It offers a modern desktop that delivers an intuitive user experience for all users – programmers and non-programmers alike.

The above lines indicate that it is an operating system used under GNU GPL and provides various distros as open-source for users.

You can use these Linux distributions on the system as your primary operating system.

- Debian

- Fedora

- Manjaro

- openSUSE

- Solus

MORE ABOUT GNOME-BASED LINUX DISTRIBUTIONS

GNOME3 is the default desktop environment on various major Linux distributions, including openSUSE, Fedora, Debian, Ubuntu, SUSE Linux Enterprise, Red Hat Enterprise Linux, CentOS, Pop!_OS, Oracle Linux, Endless OS, and Tails; as well as Solaris, a UNIX operating system. The continued fork of the last GNOME 2 release, called MATE, defaults on many Linux distros that target low usage of system resources.

It is available for installing the Linux/GNU distributions. Several distributions provide the opportunity to try their demo before we install it. Some of them are explained as follows:

What Is openSUSE?

It is an origin of the original SUSE Linux distribution and a community-based distribution in contrast to SUSE Linux Enterprise. The SUSE Company is still an influential sponsor of openSUSE. The relationship is similar to Fedora, CentOS, to Red Hat Enterprise Linux. The project uses a gecko logo to show the relationship between SUSE and openSUSE.

It is available in two flavors, the rolling-release Tumbleweed and the stable Leap. The latter is the same as Arch Linux as it is more of a "bleeding-edge" distribution with new software. You can install openSUSE as an old Linux system, but it is also available in the Windows Store for WSL. It may be neglected compared to other major Linux distributions, but it has a unique set of features and a codebase with a wealthy estate.

openSUSE also gives you access to vanilla GNOME. But unlike Fedora, it follows a much slower release schedule. You won't get access to all the latest GNOME features as soon as they are released. However, this isn't technically a bad thing. It can dedicate more time and effort to make the OS more stable and reliable by having a slow release cycle. It makes a perfect fit for professionals who can't afford to have their system crash in the middle of meaningful work.

Now, openSUSE is distributed under two release models – Leap and Tumbleweed.

Each major version is released every three years, whereas point releases or minor updates are released annually with Leap. Depending on how often you want to upgrade your system, you should pick the flavor.

The openSUSE project offers two distributions.

- Tumbleweed, which is a rolling distribution

- Leap, which is a point distribution

What Is openSUSE Used For?

It is a project that promotes the benefit of free and open-source software. It is well known for its Linux distributions, mainly Tumbleweed, a tested rolling release, and Leap, a distribution with long-term support.

However, starting and switching applications work differently from other desktop operating systems. It only uses a single panel at the top of the screen. Its session is started on Wayland. openSUSE Leap uses GNOME with Wayland as default.

What Is Fedora?

Fedora gives GNOME, and it is an Open-source Operating System built and maintained by a community using the Linux kernel architecture. We can easily install it and use it live. Workstation 33 of Fedora is available now and ships GNOME 3.38 version I Fedora, the Only Linux Distribution, creates an operating system that is free to download, use, and modify as per your needs. All the features, software, packages, and components are included inside are free. The Fedora community has thousands of volunteers, supporters, users, and contributors, who interact via various online forums, email, and wikis to support each other. It provides the latest technology on recent hardware platforms with rapid development and releases cycle.

The default desktop of Fedora is GNOME. Still, you prefer an alternative desktop environment such as KDE Plasma Desktop or Xfce. In that case, you can download a spin for your preferred desktop environment and use that to install Fedora, preconfigured for the desktop environment of your choice.

Fedora offers the latest and greatest GNOME experience out of all other Linux distros. It supports a unique ecosystem that provides users with new and updated software as soon as they are available.

With each new release of Fedora, the development team incorporates the latest version of GNOME. It allows you to access all the newly released GNOME features before anyone else.

However, since you get access to all the latest software first, there hasn't been much time to test them thoroughly. As such, be prepared to face the occasional bugs as new updates roll out. It is why Fedora is more suitable for enthusiasts and computer geeks than regular users looking for stability.

What Is Debian?

Debian is the oldest Linux distros with tons of forks and derivatives. It officially supports almost all the major Linux distros, including GNOME, which default uses.

With Debian, you will get to enjoy GNOME in its purest glory. But keep in mind that you won't get updated to the newest releases as soon as they are available, as is the case with Fedora. But at the same time, releases aren't as slow as openSUSE or CentOS.

Overall, it is a highly stable and dependable Linux distro perfect for beginners and advanced users. You will find Debian being seamlessly used by regular users to run day-to-day tasks and on web servers for hosting websites and web apps.

Also, Debian is the most massive community-run distro. When you combine that it has been around for so long, you get access to the best hardware and software compatibility.

What Is CentOS?

CentOS (Community Enterprise Operating System) is similar to open-SUSE as it focuses more on stability than delivering all the latest updates and releases. You won't get all the newest GNOME features, but you can rest assured that you rarely face bugs or system crashes.

The GNOME 3 desktop on CentOS 7 will provide a GUI for working with the Linux system. While I don't suggest using a GUI on a production server, it's a good option if you're using CentOS as a desktop.

As such, you will mostly find CentOS being used in enterprise situations. It is the most widely used platform in web hosting. It is also preferred by developers and large corporations looking for a mature and reliable OS with a longer release cycle.

What Is Arch Linux?

Arch doesn't ship with GNOME out of the box. It ships with no desktop environment at all. It is a super lightweight and flexible Linux distribution that allows you to build your own custom Linux experience with tools and software that you like.

All you need to do is install the GNOME Shell on your Arch system, and you are good to go. And since the OS doesn't come with any additional customization or extensions, you can rest assured that you will be getting the purest experience.

But that being said, you need to understand that you will need to install GNOME, and it won't be done for you. Furthermore, if anything goes wrong with the OS, you need to be knowledgeable enough to fix it yourself or find the solution through online forums.

Even installing Arch Linux can be far more intimidating than other Linux distros.

What Is Manjaro GNOME Edition?

Manjaro is based on Arch Linux and is available in many flavors – including a GNOME edition.

The beauty of Manjaro is that you are getting access to the freedom and flexibility of Arch, but with GNOME already baked in. You don't need to worry about installing GNOME and other dependencies separately, making the process much more convenient and user-friendly.

With the Manjaro GNOME edition, you are getting an up-to-date GNOME Shell desktop along with helpful software right out of the box.

But that being said, the GNOME desktop on Manjaro is slightly customized, unlike with Arch, where you can get vanilla GNOME. Furthermore, it won't update you to the latest version of GNOME as soon as it's available, and you will need to wait a couple of weeks.

What Is Pop!_OS?

Pop!_OS is based on Ubuntu and built by System76 to be distributed along their computers. But now, it's a standalone product that you can download and install on any computer, not necessarily from their manufacturers.

The best thing about Pop!_OS is that it is ready to go as soon as you install it. For example, you get straight out-of-the-box support for AMD and Nvidia GPUs – you don't need to install any drivers manually. It makes OS one of the best distros for gaming on Linux.

Like Ubuntu, it comes with a custom GNOME desktop, but it isn't as heavily skinned. On the contrary, Pop!_OS goes for a more minimal take, making GNOME feel even more sleek, intuitive, and beginner-friendly. It is why Pop!_OS is one of the most widely recommended distros for users who are just starting with Linux.

What Is Zorin OS?

It is another Ubuntu-based Linux distro designed with first-time Linux users in mind. It comes with a customized version of GNOME that allows you to switch between a Windows-like and a MacOS-like interface. Depending on which interface you pick, it will give you a familiar GUI that closely resembles the look and feel of your old OS to make the transition as seamless as possible.

You will also get access to Wine and PlayOnLinux out of the box. It allows you to run Windows applications on your Linux system, including Adobe software and the entire Microsoft Office Suite.

Thanks to Wine, all your favorite games that only have a Windows version will also run on Zorin OS, but it might not be as well optimized since it is running off a compatibility layer. It follows Ubuntu's long-term release cycle for security and stability, so you can expect a new Zorin OS version as soon as the next long-term Ubuntu release rolls out.

What Is Mageia?

We have Mageia, a fork of Mandriva Linux, currently defunct. KDE is the default desktop environment for Mageia, but you can pick GNOME as it is also officially supported, and it will give you a pure GNOME experience. It isn't as popular as the other distros on the list but is gaining popularity – the release of its latest version – Mageia 7.1, ships with tons of nifty bells and whistles. Mageia is super lightweight and easy to use for starters, making it highly beginner-friendly. But at the same time, it is also very flexible and offers tons of features that seasoned Linux users will appreciate. It supports a vast repository of software, including tons of productivity apps and games, so that you can run pretty much anything on the distro.

Furthermore, it is entirely processor agnostic, which is compatible with AMD, Intel, and even VIA processors. It is also very forgiving of your hardware configuration and will give you the best possible experience even if you are running it on limited specifications.

What Is Ubuntu?

Ubuntu 20.04 LTS version contains GNOME 3.36 with minor changes, and Ubuntu 20.10 has GNOME 3.38 version with minor changes. When we install a gnome session, we can select for launching the new GNOME through the login screen.

If you are getting into Linux, you surely must have heard about Ubuntu. It is the most popular Linux distro. It is so popular that most non-users think it is synonymous with Linux.

Back in the day, Ubuntu came out with its custom desktop environment – Unity. But, as of Ubuntu 17.10, Canonical (the developers behind Ubuntu) has switched to the GNOME Shell.

That being said, Ubuntu uses a heavily modified version of GNOME to maintain the design aesthetics of their Unity desktop. It might be a good thing for long-time Ubuntu users but isn't appreciated by users looking to get the GNOME experience as its developers intended.

System Requirements of Ubuntu GNOME

- The memory of the system should be 1.5 GB of RAM.

- The system should have a 1-GHz processor (like Intel Celeron) or better.

- Access to the Internet is helpful (to install updates during installation).

- You can use a USB port or DVD/CD drive for the installer media.

Various distros specialize in different fronts, so you can pick the one that resounds to your needs and requirements.

If you are looking for vanilla GNOME, go with Fedora or Arch, which have access to all the latest features as soon as they are released.

On the other hand, if you look for a little more stability, then Debian, openSUSE, and Mageia are perfect alternatives, with CentOS being the most stable and reliable with a long-term release cycle.

However, assume you want to stay in the middle and access new features reasonably in timely fashion without sacrificing stability. In that case, you can test out Manjaro or POP!_OS, both of which are incredibly beginner-friendly.

And finally, if you want to use GNOME because of its features and are not concerned about how it looks, go with Ubuntu or Zorin OS. Both provide you with a heavily customized GNOME desktop but are filled with valuable features and welcome new users.

HISTORY OF UBUNTU GNOME

The project started as the unofficial "remix" because a few users prioritized the GNOME 3 desktop on Unity. The 12.10 version of GNOME Quantal Quetzal was the initial version published on October 18, 2012.

The founder of Ubuntu, Mark Shuttleworth, and Canonical Executive Chairman on April 5, 2017, declared that the Ubuntu mainline version would move through Unity to the GNOME 3 desktop starting by 18.04 LTS version. It makes it identical to Ubuntu GNOME 3. After that, it was revealed that the 17.10 version of Ubuntu would be the first version for using GNOME.

In April 2017, Mark Shuttleworth specified that "Ubuntu GNOME along with the intent of distributing a fantastic each GNOME desktop and the team of Ubuntu GNOME support, not making it competitive or different with that effort." In the announcement of Ubuntu that they will switch the desktop environments via Unity to GNOME, the GNOME developers revealed on April 13, 2017, that distribution will merge within the Ubuntu, which is starting with the 17.10 release.

GNOME version 3 is now the default desktop environment on many Linux distributions, including Ubuntu, SUSE Linux, Red Hat Linux, Fedora, Debian, CentOS, Oracle Linux, Endless OS, Tail, Solaris, and a UNIX operating system. The fork of the last GNOME 2 release, called MATE.

The GNOME 1 release looked very similar to Windows 98, the current version of Microsoft Windows, a wise decision that immediately provided a familiar graphical interface for new Linux users. GNOME 1 offered desktop management and integration, not only simply window management. The files and folders can drop on the desktop, providing easy access. It was a robust advancement, and many major Linux distributions included GNOME as the default desktop. Finally, Linux had an actual desktop. We will discuss GNOME later in the other section.

Over time, GNOME continued to evolve. In 2002, GNOME 2 was a significant release. They have been cleaned up the user interface and tweaked the overall design. Instead of a single toolbar or panel at the bottom of the screen, GNOME 2 used two panels at the top and one at the bottom. The top panel included the GNOME Applications menu, an Actions menu, and shortcuts to frequently used applications. The bottom panel provided icons of running programs and a representation of the other workspaces available on the system. Using the two panels provided a cleaner user interface, separating "things you can do" (top panel) and "things you are doing" (bottom panel).

Many other users felt the same, and GNOME 2 became a standard for the Linux desktop. The successive versions made incremental improvements to GNOME's user interface, but the general design concept of "things you can do" and "things you are doing" remained the same.

Despite the success and broad appeal of GNOME, the GNOME team realized that GNOME 2 had become difficult for many to use. The application's launch menu required too many clicks. Workspaces were challenging to use. Open windows were easy to lose under piles of other application windows. In 2008, the GNOME team embarked on updating the GNOME interface. That effort produced GNOME 3.

GNOME 3 removed the traditional taskbar in favor of an Overview mode that shows all running applications. Instead of using a launch menu, users start applications with an Activities hot button in the black bar at the top. Selecting the Activities menu brings up the Overview mode, showing both things you can do with the favorite applications launcher to the left of the screen and things you are doing window representations of open applications.

Since its release, the GNOME 3 team has improved it and made it easier to use. GNOME is modern, familiar, and striking that can balance features and utility.

GNOME 1

GNOME 1 (1999)

GNOME was launched by Miguel de Icaza and Federico Mena on August 15, 1997, as a free software project and developed a desktop environment and applications for it. It was founded partly because K Desktop Environment, growing in popularity, relied on the Qt widget toolkit, which used a proprietary software license until version 2.0 (June 1999). In place of Qt, GTK (GNOME Toolkit, called GIMP Toolkit) is the base of GNOME. GTK uses the GNU GPL, a free software license that allows software linking to it to use a much more comprehensive set of permissions, including proprietary software licenses. GNOME is licensed under the LGPL for its libraries and the GNU GPL for its applications.

"GNOME is a flexible (Graphical User's Interface) that combines ease of use, the flexibility, reliability of GNU/Linux. We are extremely excited about GNOME and mean for the future of GNU/Linux computing," Miguel de Icaza, chief designer of GNOME, said earlier.

GNOME is designed to be portable to the modern UNIX system. It runs on Linux systems, BSD variants, Solaris, HP-UX, and Digital UNIX. It will be included in Red Hat and other Linux distributions such as Debian GNU/Linux and SUSE Linux.

It has features that allow users to assign an icon to a file or URL. It has a drag and drops enabled desktop, using the standard Xdnd and Motif protocols.

Its code makes it easy for international users, with core components recently supporting more than 17 languages, with more on the way. It works well with various scripting and compiling languages, including Ada, C, C++, Objective-C, TOM, Perl, Guile, etc.

"GNOME is a big step towards acquiring the Free Software Foundation's providing a whole spectrum of software from experts to end-users. We all are excited about the direction of GNOME taking us in." Richard Stallman, Founder and President of the Foundation said. "'Free Software' includes the freedom to run, copy, distribute, study, change and improve any software distributed under the General Public License. It will create an energetic environment for programmers & users to create use GNU/Linux and GNOME programs. We will see a wide range of GNOME-based applications to answer the different needs of computer users."

GNOME is available for free at http://www.gnu.org, http://www.gnome.org, and several other mirror sites. It is also included in Red Hat Software, Inc.'s GNU/Linux distributions, with other sources available in the coming years.

GNOME 2

Released in June 2002, it was very similar to a traditional desktop interface, featuring a simple desktop in which users could interact with virtual objects such as windows, icons, and files. It was started with Sawfish as its default window manager but later switched to Metacity. In GNOME 2, the concept of handling windows, applications, and files is similar to that of modern desktop operating systems. In the default configuration of GNOME version 2, the desktop has a launcher menu for rapid access to installed programs file locations; a taskbar can access open windows at the bottom of the screen. The top-right corner features a notification section for programs to display notices during running in the background. Hence, all these features can be moved to any position or orientation the user wants, replaced with other functions, or removed altogether. GNOME 2 provided similar features as the conventional desktop interface.

GNOME version 2 was the default desktop for OpenSolaris, and the MATE desktop environment is a fork of the GNOME 2 codebase.

GNOME 2.0.2 is the predecessor version of 1.0 what is the complete, accessible, and easy-to-use desktop environment. In addition to basic desktop functionality, it is a robust application framework for software developers, support for object embedding, and accessibility. GNOME 2 is part of The GNU Project and is free software.

The GNOME 2.0.2 platform includes a complete library suite to support GNOME applications. It also includes all the essential utilities for your day-to-day computing, from a simple weather monitor to a powerful file manager. GNOME 2.0.2 is compatible with several platforms, including GNU/Linux, Solaris, HP-UX, UNIX, and BSD.

The GNOME 2 development cycle allowed several features that improved performance and usability. It also includes a robust new framework that developers can leverage.

Some features are as follows:

- Improved fonts and graphics

- Usability

- Performance

- Keyboard navigation

- Accessibility

- Internationalization

- XML

Improved Font and Graphics

- Fonts can be anti-aliased (familiar graphics setting).

- There is no flicker in GTK apps.

- Images are composited onto backgrounds with the entire alpha channel, accelerated via MMX and the RENDER extension.

- There are new enhanced icons.

Usability

Streamlining, consistency, and coherence are having the primary focus of GNOME 2 Usability work.

- **Streamlining:** GNOME 2 has been simplified, and there is no need to add a pipeline. The interface clutter controlled to a GNOME where you could almost literally "do less with more." GNOME 2 removes many obscure or rarely used features. In exchange, you will find that most of the features you care about are much easier to access because a million other items do not obscure them.

- **Consistency:** Interfaces that behave according to uniform patterns are easier to learn, faster to use, and less tending to error. The GNOME Interface Guidelines have helped make the GNOME 2 interface more predictable, producing consistency between applications and promoting usable patterns within particular applications.

- **Coherence:** The GNOME 2 desktop fits nicely from "Login" to "Log Out," countless brainstorming hours and tireless hacking have produced a desktop and more than a loose confederation of modules.

Specific user-visible improvements include:

1. Menus and Panel

    - The windows can be dragged between workspaces with the Workspace Switcher applet.

    - The menus can scroll when they get too big.

    - More innovative menus accommodate diagonal mouse movements.

2. Dialogs

    - The files selector doesn't forget names when selecting a different folder.

    - The updated color and font selectors.

    - New dialog Run Program with command completion.

    - The text fields include right-clicking menus for cutting, copying, and pasting text.

3. Icons and Themes

- The new stock icons and color palette.

- It supported theming of stock icons.

- The CD Player and login screens are now themeable.

- An attractive default appearance.

4. Applications

- Everything is redesigned and easier to use Search Tool.

- The brand new lightweight help application, Yelp.

- It can control center applications for managing GNOME 2 properties have been greatly simplified and reduced in number.

- It increasing compliance with freedesktop.org standards.

- Rewritten terminal application with tabs and profiles.

- A brand new dynamic, centralized configuration system.

- Many applications have been renamed to suit their purpose better.

GNOME 3

It was released in 2011. While GNOME 1 & 2 interfaces followed the classic desktop analogy, the GNOME Shell assumed a more abstract metaphor with streamlined window management workflow unified header bar that replacing menu bar, taskbar, and toolbar and minimize and maximize buttons hidden by default.

GNOME 3 brought many enhancements to the core software. Many GNOME Core Applications went through redesigns to provide a more consistent user experience, and mutter replaced Metacity as the default window manager. Adwaita substituted Clearlooks as the default theme.

FEATURES OF GNOME

GNOME has become one of the most efficient, stable, and reliable desktops available for the Linux operating system. Not only that, it remains incredibly user-friendly. Most users have experienced regardlessly and can get up incredible speed with GNOME without applying any extra effort. So, let's look at the details of GNOME and know about its great features.

Let's take a look at its features:

- **Flatpak:** It seems like one of the best things ever happened to Linux. It lets developers distribute an app on every Linux distribution ease. The new GNOME includes GTK+ theme handling and language configuration support.

- **New Boxes Features:** Box's built-in applications can run remote and locally installed virtual machines. So, you don't need to install any virtual machine such as VMware or VirtualBox to try other Linux distros. It can automatically download operating systems from the new box assistant; all you have to do is pick the Linux distro you want to use, and Boxes will do the rest.

- **Activities Overview:** One of the essential pieces of the GNOME puzzle is the Activities overview. Activities are where you access application launchers, minimize applications, search, and virtual desktops.

- **Multimedia Apps:** Photos App has a new import feature that allows you to easily add photos to your library from SD cards and USB drives. The App can now auto-detect storage devices with new images, giving you an option to organize the pictures into albums during import itself. Other multimedia enhancements include playing MJPEG video files through a video player and reordering playlists by drag & drop in the music app. Games app has an exciting feature. It has an excellent new CRT video filter that makes game visuals look like they are being played on an old CRT TV.

- **Dash:** If you don't want application launchers on the Dash, right-click the launcher in question and select Remove from Favorites. If you like to add a favorite to the Dash, you need to open the Applications overview. To do so, click on the grid icon at the bottom of the Dash. When the Applications open, you can scroll throughout the list of installed applications to find what you are looking for. You can run that application or add it to the Dash with a single click. To add an application to the Dash, right-click the application icon, and select Add to Favorites.

- **File Manager:** Numerous improvements in Files application. This feature allows batch renaming of files. Apart from that, compressed file functionality has also been integrated into Files. Many other user interface improvements have been added as well.

- **Favorites in Files:** In Files, you can select files and folders and add them to the favorites list so that you can quickly view them in a "Starred" list, as discussed earlier. The favorite capability has also been added to the Contacts application and can pin your favorite contacts with whom you interact more.

- **Night Light:** It is the main feature in GNOME. It works as advertised, subtly adjusting the color temperature of your monitor based on the time of day. During the day you will see things as you used to. The screen temperature gets colder and brighter with more blue light – the screen transitions to a warmer hue with less blue light in the evening. The blue light filters help promote natural sleep cycles and reduce eye strain.

- **Calendar:** The month view in the Calendar in GNOME shows the Events more readable. You can also expand cells that have several events overlapped. Also, notice the weather info besides the events. The To-Do list has been revamped to reorder tasks by drag & drop.

- **Terminal:** Terminal gets some enhancements as well. Notice the redesigned preferences window. There are no longer separate Preferences, and Profile Preferences both the options are clubbed into one window. You will also see blinking text.

- **Search:** The GNOME Search tool is potent. Not only can it search for installed applications within the Application overview, but it can also search for applications not yet installed within GNOME Software and search for files.

- **GNOME Beautification:** GNOME looks more sleek and beautiful with Cantarell's enhanced default interface font. Character forms and spacing have been improved to make the text more attractive.

- **A More Wonderful Web:** The Web is the default GNOME browser and is often overlooked by users preferring to browse the Web with a better-known app, like Mozilla Firefox or Google Chrome. Bookmarking web pages on the Web now take a single click. A new bookmarks popover makes it easy to access existing bookmarks, and a new interface for managing, editing, and tagging bookmarks will appease those who like to stay organized.

- **Better Device Support:** GNOME comes with integrated Thunderbolt 3 connection support. Security checks are added to prevent data theft through unauthorized Thunderbolt 3 connections. The top bar shows the Thunderbolt 3 connection status when active. Touchpad uses a gesture for the secondary click, which is nothing but right-click action of a mouse. Keep a finger in contact with the touchpad and tap with another finger to use the motion.

- **Clocks App:** Now, adding the UTC timezone to your world times is possible.

- **Better Icons:** If there's one area where the GNOME desktop often shorts. A slate of high-resolution icons is included to ensure that everything looks sharp and detailed on high-density displays. Many redesigned devices, mime-type, and app icons feature a brighter, cleaner, and more modern look.

- **App "Usage":** GNOME ships with a new technology preview app called Usage. Using this App, you can see CPU and RAM consumption and highlighted problem areas. It is a great feature that helps you troubleshoot issues quicker than before. More features are planned in future updates to the App.

- **Screenshots:** Another great feature is built-in screenshot support. Driven by hotkeys, it allows you to capture the whole screen, an active window, or a screen region to the clipboard or directly to a PNG file under $HOME\Pictures\Screenshot-*.

- **All-New On-Screen Keyboard:** The On-screen keyboard has been re-coded entirely in GNOME. The new keyboard is user-friendly and automatically pops up when a text is selected. The view gets away to ensure you can see what you are typing.

- **Minimalist Design:** Most interfaces include quite a few on-screen elements unrelated to the task at hand. Windows & Chromebooks have taskbars across the bottom that contain all the favorite or open apps. On GNOME, the panel at the top does not contain any app launchers. The panel is small and black, like on a phone or tablet. It includes the date and time a few system indicators in the top right.

GNOME SHELL

It is the graphical shell of the GNOME desktop environment starting with version GNOME 3, released on April 6, 2011. It provides essential functions like launching applications, switching between windows, and a widget engine. GNOME Shell replaced GNOME Panel and some ancillary components of GNOME 2.

GNOME Shell is written in C and JavaScript as a plugin for Mutter.

In contrast to the KDE Plasma Workspaces, a software framework intended to facilitate the creation of multiple graphical shells for different devices, the GNOME Shell is designed to be used on desktop computers with large screens operated via keyboard and mouse, as well as portable computers with smaller screens operated via their keyboard, touchpad, or touchscreen. However, a fork of the GNOME Shell, known as Phish, was created in 2018 for specialization with touchscreen smartphones.

History

The first version of GNOME Shell was created during GNOME's User Experience Hackfest 2008 in Boston.

After the traditional GNOME desktop and accusations of stagnation and low concept, the resulting meeting led to GNOME 3.0 in April 2009, since Red Hat has been the main driver of GNOME Shell's development.

Prerelease versions of GNOME Shell were first made available in August 2009 and became a regular, non-default part of GNOME in version 2.28 in September 2009. It was finally shipped as GNOME's default user interface on April 6, 2011.

Software Architecture

GNOME Shell is integrated with Mutter, a compositing window manager, and Wayland compositor. It is based on Clutter to provide visual effects and hardware acceleration. According to GNOME Shell maintainer Owen Taylor, it is set up as a Mutter plugin primarily written in JavaScript and uses GUI widgets provided by GTK+ version 3.

Features

The changes to the user interface (UI) include, but are not limited to:

- Support clutter and Mutter multi-touch gestures.

- Support for HiDPI monitors.

- A new Activities overview, which houses:

  1. A dock or Dash is used for quickly switching between and launching applications.

  2. A window selector, similar to macOS's Mission Control, also incorporates a workspace switcher/manager.

  3. An application picker.

  4. Search

- "Snapping" windows to screen borders makes them fill up half of the screen or the whole screen.

- By default, a single-window button, Close, instead of three.

- The minimization option has been removed due to the lack of a panel to minimize. Maximization can be accomplished using the window above snapping or double-clicking the window title bar.

It provides core interface functions like launching applications, switching windows, or seeing notifications. It has the advantage of the capabilities of modern graphics hardware and introduces innovative user interface concepts to provide a delightful and easy-to-use experience. GNOME Shell is the technology of the GNOME 3 user experience.

A fallback mode is offered in versions 3.0–3.6 for those without hardware acceleration which offers the GNOME Panel desktop. The method can also be toggled through the System Settings menu. GNOME 3.8 removed the fallback mode and replaced it with GNOME Shell extensions that offer a more traditional look and feel.

GNOME Shell has the following graphical and functional elements:

- Top bar

- System status area

- Activities overview

- Dash

- Window picker

- Application picker

- Search

- Notifications and messaging tray

- Application switcher

- Indicators tray

Extensibility

GNOME Shell's functionality can be changed with extensions, which can be written in JavaScript. Users can find and install extensions using the GNOME extensions website. Some of these extensions are hosted in GNOME's git repository, though they are not official.

GNOME 3: PROS AND CONS

Anyone who switches to GNOME 3 is both an opportunity and a distraction. On the one hand, it is the opportunity to put aside some annoying behaviors in earlier GNOME releases. On the other hand, GNOME 3 is a distraction because its changes can get in the way of long-established work methods.

As a result, you need to look at GNOME 3's pros and cons before deciding to make the new desktop part of your everyday computing unless, of course, you are the sort that automatically rejects or embraces change simply because it is unique.

GNOME 3 contains many changes. For example, you might see that improved hardware interaction that GNOME 3 offers a Suspend option only on a machine that supports that option. Such enhancements are easy to overlook and, despite their convenience, too minor to create a large part of anybody's reaction to GNOME 3.

Here are various pros and cons of the new desktop that might be important for you.

Pros

- **A standard interface:** The earlier GNOME releases were designed with the workstation and the laptop in mind. That is no longer realistic in this age of netbooks, tablets, and mobile devices. GNOME 3 is designed for all users.

- In the GNOME 2 series, the system settings menu of alphabetized items is divided into Personal and Administration sub-menus. GNOME 3 reduces inefficiency with a window of settings organized by category that is easier and quicker to scan.

- GNOME 3 replaces the menu with a list of applications on the Activities overview screen. These changes allow larger icons and eliminate the problem of editing to keep it short at the risk of effectively hiding items from users.

- Improved Display of Virtual Workspaces.

- On the right of the Activities is a visual display of all open workspaces that show the running applications. It is a marked improvement over earlier GNOME releases.

- The most significant advantage of GNOME 3 is most likely to be resisted. Hence, GNOME 3 makes several advanced features more prominent and easier to use.

- The Dash on the Activities displays your favorites more prominently while switching between screens encourages learning keyboard shortcuts.

- GNOME 3 allows you to move to a messaging window without switching the focus.

Cons

- GNOME 3 doesn't allow icons on the desktop. It depends on the distribution. That will be irrelevant for half of the users, but this limitation will be a deal-breaker for the other half. You can learn to edit Gconf – and, so far, I haven't found any instructions on the Web – they will either have to learn to live without icons or hunt for a new distribution.

- You can switch to the Activities screen to open applications. Selecting an application that immediately changes you to the workspace means that you have to switch back to the Activities page to open any application you want to run simultaneously. The limitation also exists in the classic menu of the GNOME 2 series, but it requires far more mouse clicks in GNOME 3.

CHAPTER SUMMARY

In this chapter, we have discussed the basic knowledge of the GNOME desktop environment and also covered the other GNOME-based Distros like Fedora, openSUSE, Ubuntu, Zorin OS, and Majora Edition. You will get to know about GNOME versions, history, and simple, useful terms like GUI, CLI, and TUI.

CHAPTER 2

GNOME Installation

IN THIS CHAPTER

- ➤ GNOME desktop environment
- ➤ GNOME features
- ➤ Beyond basic customization
- ➤ GNOME Classic
- ➤ GNOME on Xorg
- ➤ Ubuntu on Wayland
- ➤ What is a GNOME shell extension?

Now we will learn how to install the GNOME desktop environment on a computer running an Ubuntu Linux system. The latest versions of Ubuntu use Unity as the default desktop environment. GNOME allows to use of a different desktop environment with a different layout and features like search optimization, improved graphics rendering, and built-in Google Docs support.

GNOME DESKTOP ENVIRONMENT

Install GNOME and GNOME Shell Extensions on Ubuntu

GNOME is the default desktop environment for Ubuntu. If you don't have a desktop environment installed or have a different background, you would like to switch to GNOME.

DOI: 10.1201/9781003311942-2

GNOME includes various desktop applications, and it aims to make a Linux system easy to use for nonprogrammers. This section will help you how to install the GNOME desktop environment on Ubuntu.

Install GNOME Minimal on Ubuntu 20.04

The "Vanilla GNOME" is a clean GNOME version desktop installation. It lacks the Software you would expect as default; however, the minimal desktop resource requirements.

To install the minimal desktop environment of GNOME, use the system's package manager to install the GUI, and the gdm3 manager runs the following command:

```
$ sudo apt install gnome-session gdm3
```

After installation, reboot your system; you will be presented with a GNOME login.

```
$ reboot
```

The easiest way to install an entire GNOME desktop is by using the tasksel command. First, ensure that the tasksel command is available on your system:

```
$ sudo apt install tasksel
```

Next, use the tasksel command to install GNOME desktop:

```
$ sudo tasksel install ubuntu-desktop
```

All done; now reboot your Ubuntu system:

```
$ sudo reboot
```

Install GNOME entire desktop on Ubuntu 20.04

The "Full version" of GNOME will come with Software by default. Some users may find it not handy, and others may find that it comes with all the necessary things they need. Remember that this version will consume more system resources than the minimal version.

Here are the steps to install GNOME on your Ubuntu system:

- Open a Terminal on the Ubuntu system. Click the Dash icon on the top left and select Terminal from your app list to open the Terminal, or you can do this Ctrl + Alt + T on your keyboard to open the Terminal.

- Type command Sudo apt-get update in Terminal then hit enter, and the command will update all your repositories and ensure you have the latest versions of packages.

```
user@user-VirtualBox:~$ sudo apt-get update
[sudo] password for user:
Hit:1 http://in.archive.ubuntu.com/ubuntu focal
InRelease
Hit:2 http://in.archive.ubuntu.com/ubuntu focal-
updates InRelease
Hit:3 http://in.archive.ubuntu.com/ubuntu focal-
backports InRelease
Hit:4 http://security.ubuntu.com/ubuntu focal-security
InRelease
Hit:5 https://dl.google.com/linux/chrome/deb stable
InRelease
Reading package lists... Done
```

- Next, type command Sudo apt-get installs ubuntu-GNOME-desktop, and this command will install the whole GNOME desktop environment with the standard applications and optimizations for Ubuntu.

- Alternatively, you can install the GNOME Shell using the sudo apt-get install GNOME-shell command. It will install the minimal packages required for the GNOME desktop environment, excluding the additional desktop apps and Ubuntu themes that come with the complete installation.

- The ubuntu-GNOME-desktop install, which already includes GNOME Shell to make sure, you can even combine the two commands and type sudo apt-get install GNOME-shell ubuntu-GNOME-desktop.

  Syntax,

```
$ sudo apt-get install ubuntu-GNOME-desktop
```

The output of the above-given command will be

```
user@user-VirtualBox:~$ sudo apt-get install
ubuntu-gnome-desktop
[sudo] password for user:
Reading package lists... Done
Building dependency tree
Reading state information... Done
The following additional packages will be installed:
  adwaita-icon-theme-full fonts-cantarell gnome-session
The following NEW packages will be installed:
  adwaita-icon-theme-full fonts-cantarell gnome-
session ubuntu-gnome-desktop
0 upgraded, four newly installed, 0 to remove, and
five not upgraded.
We need to get 7,203 kB of archives.
```

While the installation, you will be prompted to upgrade other packages. Type "y" and Enter to proceed with the install.

You can try this command too to install GNOME in your system.
   Syntax sudo apt install gnome,

```
$ sudo apt install gnome
```

Or

```
$ sudo apt install gnome-s
```

You will see an output on screen like this,

```
user@user-VirtualBox:~$ sudo apt install gnome
[sudo] password for user:
Reading package lists... Done
Building dependency tree
Reading state information... Done
gnome is already the newest version (1:3.30+2).
The following packages were automatically installed
and are no longer required:
  linux-headers-5.11.0-43-generic
linux-hwe-5.11-headers-5.11.0-43
  linux-image-5.11.0-43-generic
linux-modules-5.11.0-43-generic
  linux-modules-extra-5.11.0-43-generic
Use 'sudo apt autoremove' to remove them.
```

It takes some time to install properly.

- After your installation is finished, restart your computer to start using your Ubuntu system with the GNOME desktop environment.

When you see your screen after restarting your system, it seems like it is the same as before, but there will be a small icon in the bottom left corner. When you hit that icon, you will see a window pops up right away as shown in the following figure.

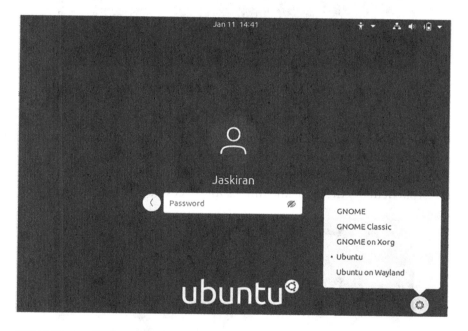

GNOME installation Window.

Choose any of your working environments desktop, whether it is GNOME, GNOME Classic, or GNOME on Xorg, Ubuntu, or Wayland.

Select any of the desktop environments to use now; you need to login, enter your password, and your system is ready. So the first desktop environment is GNOME, which will help you get into it, then you will see a beautiful interface on the screen as shown in the following figure.

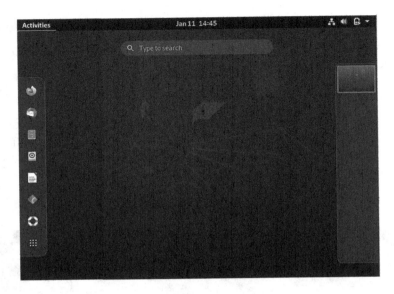

Desktop environment GNOME interface.

We are using GNOME 3.36 in our Ubuntu system. GNOME 3.36: "Gresik." It contains six months of work by the GNOME community and includes many improvements, performance enhancements, and new features.

Highlights include visual refreshes for several applications and interfaces, particularly the login and unlock interfaces (see the following figure).

Login Screen of GNOME desktop.

GNOME 3.36 was released on March 11, 2020, and features all the improvements as mentioned below. That said, be aware that some Linux distro packagers disable, tweak, or change things to suit their user base, so allow for some differences.

This section rounds up the best improvements, changes, and features that the latest GNOME desktop environment ships with and distill them into an easily scan able list.

GNOME FEATURES

- Theme Improvements
- "Do Not Disturb" Toggle
- Respects System Fonts
- New Extensions App
- New Lock Screen
- New Shell Dialogs
- Password Peeking
- Software Updates
- App Folder Tweaks
- Tweaks to Settings
- more

Let's discuss each of them in detail.

Improved GNOME Shell Theme: We saw the updated GNOME Shell theme earlier, and we are happy to say that all of the significant visual enhancements are present here in GNOME 3.36.

Although some UI changes are small and subtle, meaning that you might not notice them at all, other changes are far more apparent and harder to miss that.

Have a look at the new and improved notification calendar tray where calendar, weather, and world clock widgets that show up make much better use of available space. They also support a carded appearance due to a drop shadow effect (see the following figure).

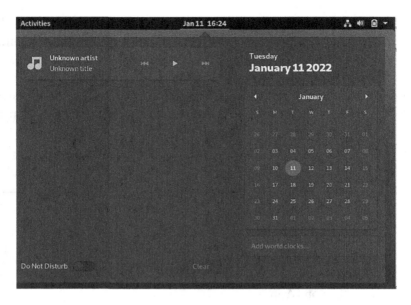

Improved GNOME Shell theme.

Notifications show more notable icons yet somehow look more compact than before. And notifications listed in the message tray now use the same cool "carded" styling as other UI elements, improving consistency throughout the GNOME Shell UI (see the following figure).

Notification icons on GNOME.

Search results in the view screen have been made neater and more organized. These tweaks should make searching easier to "spot" the correct result.

Do Not Disturb the Toggle: If you don't want that other application notifications or alerts to disturb you while working on a code project, watching a film, or doing stuff. The GNOME has an excellent option to handle all the interrupted stuff. The notification/calendar tray has added an easy-to-access "do not disturb" toggle. Anytime you want to stop screen-stealing toasts from popping up, open the notification shade and hit the new Do Not Disturb switch (see the following figure).

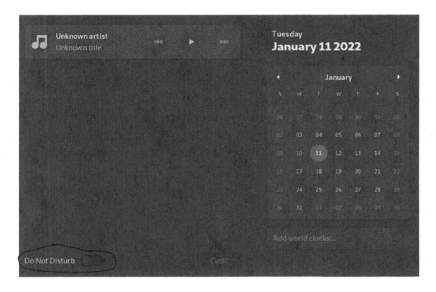

Do not disturb the toggle.

Font Settings: GNOME 3.36 has made changes to the "interface font" setting. It means you can change the GNOME Shell font to anything you like without manually editing hidden .css files, but directly via the GNOME Tweaks app. It is a slight but long-overdue personalization boost.

GNOME Tweak Tool changes the font family and size for applications windows, interface, and terminal. Still, these changes do not modify the font used in the GNOME top bar, notifications, extension menus, the date/time dropdown, the Dash/Activities overlay, etc.

The GNOME Tweak Tool is used in the intersection with the GNOME Shell to modify its interface. In other words, it is used to alter the look and feel of your Ubuntu system.

Here are some helpful GNOME Shell themes you can use to customize your GNOME DE:

1. Prof-GNOME-theme

2. Orchis GTK theme

3. Nordic

4. Big Sur

5. Yaru-Colors

6. Layan GTK Theme

7. Ultimate Dark

Prof-GNOME *Theme*: It is one of the popular GNOME themes. If you are looking for a light-weight desktop, then this theme will not disappoint.

It features two major color variants: light and dark. However, it does offer a variation of the light and dark theme, making the UI elements stand out clearly, giving this theme a very classy-looking touch and feel.

The theme is compatible with GTK 3/4, allowing you to use it even on modern GNOME Desktop versions.

It has various sub-themes such as:

• Prof-GNOME-Dark-3.2 to 3.6

• Prof-GNOME-Darker-3.0 to 3.3

• Prof-GNOME-Darker-3.4.1 to 3.6

• Prof-GNOME-Light-3.0 to 3.3

• Prof-GNOME-Light-3.4.1 to 3.6

• Prof-GNOME-Light-DS-3.0 to 3.3

• Prof-GNOME-Light-DS-3.4.1 to 3.6

• Prof-GNOME-Variant-2.0

• Prof-GNOME-theme 1.1 to 2.2

• GNOME-professional-40-dark

- GNOME-professional-40.1

- GNOME-professional-solid-40.1-dark

- GNOME-professional-solid-40.1

Orchis GTK Theme: It is a compatible and straightforward theme in various color variants, including light, dark, light compact, dark compact, and many more.

Orchis Color Options: Besides the rounded-off, semi-flat look and style, the theme also has a stylish, minimal, and appealing look that you can customize further using icon packs such as Tela Icons. The Orchis theme also comes packaged with a simple bash script installer. This makes the installation reasonably straightforward.

You can install the theme from the Snap Store or by running,

```
$ sudo snap install orchis-themes
```

Nordic Theme: Nordic is a Gtk3.20+ based theme implemented with the Nordic color palette. It gives a very minimalistic and complementary look with its dark color scheme.

The Nordic theme also offers variants, including different color accents. It provides a shell and applications theme, making it look natural.

Install the Nordic GTK Theme: The Nordic GTK theme is available on Github. To get this theme set up, you must install the Git package on your PC. To do that, open up a terminal window by pressing Ctrl + Alt + T or Ctrl + Shift + T on the keyboard. Then, when the terminal is open, follow the command line instructions below:

- For Ubuntu

  ```
  $ sudo apt install git
  ```

- For Debian

  ```
  $ sudo apt-get install git
  ```

- For Arch Linux

  ```
  $ sudo pacman -S git
  ```

- For Fedora

  ```
  $ sudo dnf install git
  ```

- For openSUSE

  ```
  $ sudo zypper install git
  ```

Big Sur Theme: If you are looking for a macOS feel, we have the best theme for you. The Big Sur theme borrows heavily on the look of the new macOS Big Sur release. It comes in light and dark color variants, allowing you to complement the GNOME Desktop with a new feel, animations, and a blurry effect. The theme also supports GTK 3/4. When paired with the perfect icon pack, this theme is unparalleled.

Compatible with:

- Deepin
- KDE
- GNOME
- ElementaryOs
- Xfce4

Yaru-Colors Theme: If you want to give your GNOME system the classic Ubuntu desktop feel and look, the Yaru theme is your best bet.

The Yaru-Colors GTK shell theme offers varying color scheme options, recolored cursors and icons, an Ubuntu-style dock, and snap and folder color change support.

It also has a complimentary icon theme to spruce up those old GNOME-looking icons. It is compatible and minimalistic, allowing you to customize your desktop without messing up the overall functionality.

Yaru-Colors themes contain the following:

1. GTK 2/3 theme

2. GNOME-Shell theme

3. Recolored icons (more information below)

4. Recolored cursors

5. Ubuntu-Dock theme (indicators)

6. Unity support (brought with Yaru 20.04)

7. Wallpapers (see below) Please note: I've added Yarus source files for gtk2/3, GNOME-shell, Unity, icons, and cursors to my git to be able to work with them.

New "Extensions" App: GNOME 3.36 extensions allow you to add new features to GNOME Shell, tame a particular quirk or make the desktop environment work the way you want it to.

GNOME shell extensions are managed using a new Extensions app rather than Software. The Extensions app updates extensions, configures extension preferences, and removes or disables unwanted extensions.

So it's nice to see GNOME developers are embracing extensions in this release by morphing the little-used and hidden GNOME-extensions-pref panel into a new, fully-furnished tool: the GNOME Extensions app. The new GNOME Extensions app can enable/disable extensions that you install from the extensions.gnome.org website; install/apply extension updates, and provide easier access to extension settings.

GNOME Shell 3.36 even checks for extension updates on start-up and will install/apply an update if needed. It means you will always be running the latest versions of whichever add-ons you use nice! You don't need to do anything special to "get" the app either. It is available by default wherever GNOME Shell is running.

New Lock Screen: For GNOME's new screen login and lock screen way back in 2018, and peased to report that GNOME 3.36 includes a new lock screen.

The lock screen works the same way: a lock screen "shield" shows the time, date, and any other pending notifications, smush a button, click on the shield screen to reveal a password input field.

There are no longer two separate screens; the password fields appear on the same screen as the time and date one.

GNOME's new lock screen has a blurred version of the desktop wallpaper, a design change that allows for improved typography while the user avatar pod has been restructured.

New Shell Dialogs: An effective dose of consistency is apparent in the various dialog prompts throughout the Shell UI, e.g., when powering off, being prompted to enter a password, using the Wi-Fi network selector, etc. All elements in core system dialogs, e.g., title, explanation, password field, etc., are now center-aligned. Icons are no longer used, and hint text is used in place of sub-headings; for example, "enter password" is inside the password entry field.

App Folder Changes: GNOME 3.34 brought the ability to create app folders directly in the application launcher. It's so easy to use: you drag and drop apps onto each other to create new folders.

Although a handy feature, app folders come with a few visual quirks, and the "rearranging icons" animation needed a bit of ironing out. In GNOME 3.36, the app folders feature is tightened up. There's now a more attentive and predictable animation when dragging app icons in/out of folders, while drag and drop and paging actions are more responsive. App folders themselves are now treated as dialogs.

A Guided Tour of the Ubuntu GNOME Desktop

Ubuntu 20.04 includes the GNOME 3 desktop environment. Although lacking the complexity of Windows and macOS desktops, GNOME 3 provides an uncluttered and intuitive desktop environment that provides all of the essential features of a windowing environment with the added advantage that it can be learned quickly.

In this section, the features of the GNOME desktop will be covered together with an outline of how basic tasks are performed and also tell about some of the fundamental components of the desktop. These components include Windows, Workspaces, and Applications. Almost all the work that you do in GNOME will involve these very basic components.

Of all the GNOME environment desktops available for the Linux operating system, it has become one of the most efficient, stable, and reliable while remaining incredibly user-friendly. Most users, regardless of experience, can get up to speed with GNOME with next to no effort.

The screen shown in shows the appearance of a typical, newly launched GNOME desktop session before any other programs have been launched or configuration changes made. The main desktop area is where you will see when applications and other utilities are launched.

The top bar of the screen is called the top bar. It includes the Activities menu, the daytime, a collection of buttons and icons, network status, audio volume, battery power, another status, and account settings. The currently active application on the desktop also appears in the top bar. For example, it shows the application menu for the Terminal program (see the following figure).

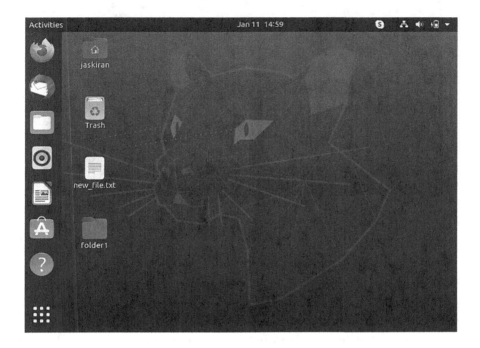

Desktop environment Ubuntu.

Activities Overview

One of the essential components of the GNOME puzzle is the Activities overview. Activities are where you access application launchers, minimize applications, search, and virtual desktops. To get to the summary of activities, you can do one of the following:

- Click on the Activities in the upper left corner

- Hover mouse cursor in the upper left corner

- Click the Super (Windows) key on your keyboard; the activities will be shown (see the following figure).

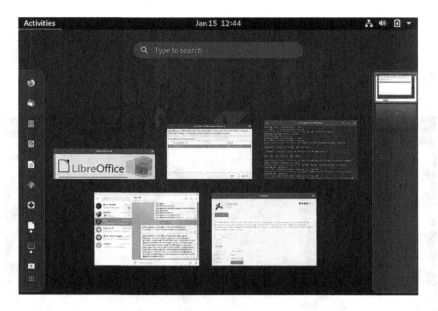

Activities overview.

The Dash

The Activities overview houses a few critical components to the GNOME desktop. If you look on the top left corner of the Activities window, you'll notice a bar of icons called The Dash. The Dash contains your Favorite launchers for applications you often use. Out of the box, you will find launchers from top to bottom, for Firefox (as the web browser), Evolution (as email/calendar), Rhythmbox (as a music player), GNOME Photos (as Photo viewer), Files (as a file manager), and GNOME Software (as app store). Click any of those icons to launch its associated application.

If you don't want application launchers on the Dash, right-click the launcher in question and select Remove from Favorites.

Application Overview

Click on the grid icon (nine dots) at the bottom of the Dash to reach this tool. When the overview of Applications opens, you can scroll the list of installed applications to find what you are looking for. You can launch any application or add it to the Dash with a single click.

To add an application to the Dash overview, locate the application, right-click the application icon, and select Add to Favorites.

After adding an application launcher to Favorites, it will automatically be added to the Dash, where you can launch the application without opening the Applications overview (see the following figure).

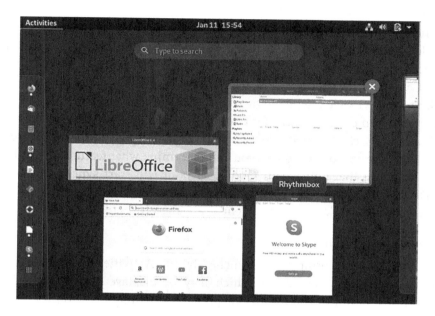

Desktop environment GNOME application interface.

Search

Note that the list can filter to display all applications or only those used by selecting the buttons at the bottom center of the screen. It is essential to be aware that some entries are folders holding additional applications.

An alternative to browsing the applications is to search using the search bar that appears when the Activities menu is clicked. The list of matches will refine as the text is typed into the search box. To add an application to the dash for more convenient access, locate the icon for the application, right-click on it, and select the Add to the Favorites menu option.

The GNOME Search tool is potent; not only can it search for installed applications within the Application overview, but it can also search for applications not yet installed within GNOME Software and search for files. To explain this, suppose you've created a file (by the LibreOffice office) called my_file.odt. If you open the Dash and then type life, you will see my newly created file and related applications.

Click on the entry you're looking for, and it will open.

Right-click on the icon to remove an app from the dash and select Remove from Favorites.

Calendar and Notifications

Click on the clock icon in the middle of the top bar to reveal the integrated calendar and notifications. If there is any notification available, give it a click to act on it.

Calendars, the process is simple if you want to sync your GNOME calendar to your Google calendar. Open the Dash and type online in the search bar and then click the entry for Online Accounts. In the consequent window (below), click Google and then walk through the account add wizard.

Once the account is added, you can determine what features are to be included. At that point, your Google account will start syncing to your GNOME desktop. If you open up the Evolution groupware suite, you will see that the Google email and calendar are already there, ready for use.

Launching Activities

Applications and utilities are launched by the Activities overview dashboard (refer to as the dash), which may be displayed by clicking the Activities button in the top bar or pressing the unique key on the keyboard. On Windows keyboards, this is the Windows key. The key displays a magnifying glass on macOS, the Command key, and Chromebooks.

By default, the dash displays an icon for a predefined collection of commonly used applications and an icon for applications currently running. If the application is presently running, its icon appears with a dot marker to the left of the icon, and if multiple copies are running, a dot will appear for each instance.

Click on the application icon in the dash to launch an application.

To find an application not included on the dash, there is an option to select the bottom-most icon (the square comprising nine dots) to display a browsable list of applications.

Managing Windows

When many application windows are open, the Super + Tab keyboard shortcut displays the switcher panel allowing a different window to be chosen as the currently active window.

To cycle backward via the icons in the switcher, use the Shift + Tab keyboard shortcut.

Using Workspaces

That screen where the app windows appear in the workspace, and GNOME 3 allows multiple workspaces to be configured. To create a new workspace, display the Activities overview and move the mouse pointer to the far right of the screen to display the workspaces panel.

To switch to a different panel, select it from the list. To move a window from one workspace, display the workspaces panel and drag and drop the application window onto the destination workspace. When a window is added to a blank workspace, another empty workspace is added to the workspace panel, creating multiple workspaces.

To remove a workspace, either close all the windows on that workspace or move them to another workspace.

Calendar and Notifications

When the system needs to notify of an event, a popup will appear at the top of the workspace. Any previous notifications are available by clicking on the day and time in the top bar to access the calendar.

Desktop Settings

To access the Settings application, click on the down arrow on the far right of the top bar and select the button with the tools icon as highlighted.

The Settings provides a wide range of Ethernet and Wi-Fi connections, screen background customization options, screen locking, power management controls, and language preferences. To explore the settings available in each category, select an option from the left-hand panel in the Settings window.

The menu also includes options to switch users, adjust audio volume, change to a different Wi-Fi network, and log out, restart, or power off the system.

Panels

The panels are two bars that run the top and bottom of the screen. By default, the top panel shows the GNOME main menu bar, the date-time, and the launcher for the GNOME help system, and the bottom the panel shows you the list of open windows and the workspace switcher.

Panels can customize to contain various tools, such as other menus and launchers and small utility applications, called panel applets. For example, you can configure your panel to display the current weather for your location.

Windows

Most applications run inside more than one window. You can display various windows on the Desktop at the simultaneous. Windows can resize and move around to accommodate workflow. Each has a title bar at the top with buttons that allow you to minimize, maximize, and close the window.

Workspaces

You can subdivide the Desktop into separate workspaces. Each workspace can contain different windows, allowing you to group-related tasks.

File Manager

The Nautilus file manager provides access to files, folders, and applications and also can manage the contents of folders in the file manager and open the files in the appropriate applications.

Preferences

You can customize the Desktop using the preference tools. Each tool can control a particular part of the behavior of the Desktop. These tools find in the Preferences submenu of the Desktop top-level menu on your panel.

Customizing the Dash

The Dash's size, position, and behavior may be changed from within the Settings app by selecting the Appearance option.

The position can be set to any of the four sides of the screen, while the Icon size can be used to reduce the size of the dock. Finally, if enabled, the auto-hide dock option will cause the dock to recede from view until the mouse pointer moves to the edge of the screen where it is currently located.

Switching to Dark Mode

In dock settings, the Appearance panel of the Settings app allows the desktop to be switched between light, standard, and dark modes. For example, it shows the dark mode selected.

Installing Ubuntu Software

In common with other operating systems such as macOS, Windows, iOS, and Android, Ubuntu has an "App Store" in the Ubuntu Software tool.

It provides you with a list of applications available for installation based on recommendations, categories, and editor's picks. Available applications may also be searched to find a specific item.

To install an application, select it in the Ubuntu Software window and click on the Install button.

BEYOND BASIC CUSTOMIZATION

GNOME 3 has a clean and uncluttered environment with minimal customization options. However, that does not mean that it is not possible to make additional changes to the desktop. The GNOME Project has developed a GNOME Tweaks tool for this very purpose. Use the following commands to install and run this tool.

```
$ apt install gnome-tweaks
$ gnome-tweaks
```

Once GNOME Tweaks has loaded, the interface shown will appear.

A range of options for customizing the desktop is now available to cover in this chapter so take some time to experiment with these settings before proceeding to the next chapter.

Windows

It is a rectangular-shaped area of the screen, with a border all around and a title bar at the top. Each window displays an application, permitting you to have more than a single application to perform various tasks simultaneously. You can think of windows as pieces of paper on your desktop: for example, they can overlap or be side by side. You can control a window's position on the screen, as well as its size. You can manage which windows overlap other windows, so the one you want to work with is obvious. An application has one main window and opens additional windows at the user's request. The rest of this section describes the different types of windows and how you can interact with them.

Types of Windows

There are three main types of windows:

- **Application windows:** It allows all the minimize, maximize, and close operations through the buttons on the title bar. When opening an application, you will usually see a window of this type appear.

- **Dialog windows:** It appears at the request of an application window. A dialog window alerts a problem, then asks for confirmation of an action or request input from you.

- **Manipulating windows:** You can also alter the size and position of windows on the screen. It allows you to see more than one application and do different tasks simultaneously. For example, you might want to read text on a web page and write with a word processor; or a simple change to another application to do a different task or see the progress.

Workspaces

It allows you to manage windows that are on your screen. You can suppose your workspaces as virtual screens, which can switch between at any time. Every workspace can contain the same desktop, panels, and menus. However, you can run various applications and open other windows in each workspace. The applications in each workspace remain there, and you can switch to other workspaces. By default, four workspaces are available where you can switch between them with the Workspace Switcher applet at the right of the bottom panel. It shows a representation of your workspaces, by default a row of four rectangles. Click on one to switch to that workspace. "Workspaces Displayed in Workspace Switcher," Workspace Switcher contains four workspaces. The first three workspaces have open windows. The last workspace does not have open windows. The presently active workspace is highlighted.

Applications

An application is a computer program that allows performing a particular task. You use applications to create text documents such as letters or reports; to work with spreadsheets; to listen to favorite music; to navigate the Internet, or create, edit, or view images and videos. For each of these tasks, you can use a different application. Choose the application to launch an application from the applications menu.

The applications of GNOME include the following:

- Gedit Text Editor is used to read, create, or modify any simple text without formatting.

- Dictionary allows one to look up definitions of a word.

- Image Viewer can display single image files and extensive image collections.

- Calculator [ghelp:gcalctool] performs basic, financial, and scientific calculations.

- Character Map can choose letters and symbols from the Unicode character set and paste them into any other application.

- Nautilus File Manager displays folders and their contents and uses them to copy, move, classify your files, access CDs, USB flash drives, or any removable media.

The Terminal

It gives access to the system command line.

GNOME applications include games, music and video players, a web browser, software tools, and utilities to manage the system. GNOME applications, such as a word processor, graphics editor.

All GNOME applications have many features in common, making it easier to learn how to work with a new GNOME application.

Standard Features

The applications provided with the GNOME share several characteristics. For example, the applications have a consistent look. The applications share characteristics because they use the same programming libraries that use the standard GNOME programming libraries are called the GNOME-compliant application. For example, Nautilus and the gedit text editor are GNOME applications. The libraries enable GNOME to run existing applications and GNOME-compliant applications. For instance, if your system is UNIX-based, you can run current X11 and Motif applications from the GNOME Desktop. GNOME-compliant application features are as follows.

Consistent look GNOME-compliant applications have a consistent look-and-feel. GNOME-compliant applications use the look and feel settings specified in the preference tools.

You can use the tools to change the look of GNOME applications:

- Menus and toolbars preference tool

- Theme preference tool

- Menu bars, toolbars, and status bars

Most GNOME applications have a menu bar, a toolbar, and a status bar. The menu bar always contains a File menu and a Help menu. The File menu always includes a Quit menu item, and the Help menu always consists of an about a menu item. A toolbar appears under the menu bar. A toolbar contains buttons for the most used commands. A status bar at the bottom of a window provides information about what you are viewing in the window. GNOME-compliant applications might also contain other bars. For example, Nautilus includes a location bar.

Some of the bars in GNOME applications are detachable that handle can grab and drag to another location. You can remove the bar to snap to another side of the window or another part of the screen. For example, you can detach the menu bar, toolbar, and location bar in the file manager.

Default Shortcut Keys

GNOME applications use the duplicate shortcut keys to perform the same actions. For example, to quit a GNOME-compliant application, press Ctrl-Q. To undo a step in a GNOME-compliant application, press Ctrl-Z.

Drag-and-Drop

GNOME applications use the same protocol to use the drag-and-drop operations. Therefore, GNOME applications provide consistent feedback when you drag-and-drop items.

This part gives you the information you need to log in to and shut down GNOME, and to start, manage, and end a desktop session.

Starting a Session

A session is a period you spend using GNOME. During a session, you open any applications, print, browse the web browser, and so on.

Logging in to GNOME begins once the session. The login screen of GNOME is the gateway to the GNOME Desktop, where you enter your username and password and select options such as the language you want GNOME to use for your session. Usually, logging out ends the session, but you can choose to save the state of your session and restore.

Next time you can use GNOME, then see the section called "Sessions Preferences."

Logging in to GNOME

To log in to a GNOME session, perform the following steps:

1. On the login screen, click on the Session icon. Choose the GNOME Desktop from the list of available desktop environments.

2. Enter username in the Username field on the login screen, then press Return.

3. Enter the password in the Password field on the login screen, then press Return.

When you log in successfully, you will see a splash informing you of GNOME's steps to start up. When GNOME is ready and you will see the Desktop and begin using your computer.

The first time you log in, the session manager starts a new session. If you have logged in before, then the session manager restores your previous session if you saved the settings in the prior session when you logged out. If you want to shut or restart the system before logging in, click on the System icon on the login screen. A dialog is displayed. Select the option that you require, then click OK.

GNOME CLASSIC

What Is GNOME Classic?

It is a feature for users who want a more traditional desktop experience. GNOME Classic desktop is based on GNOME 3 technologies. It changes the user interface such as the Applications, Places menus on the top bar and a window list at the bottom of the screen.

You can use the Application on the top bar to launch applications. The Activities is available by selecting the Activities item from the menu. You can press the Super key to open an activities overview to get the Activities overview.

Window List

The window list located at the bottom of the screen provides access to all the open windows and applications and allows you quickly minimize and restore them.

GNOME displays an identifier for the current working workspace at the right-hand side of the window list such as 1 for the top workspace. Extra, the identifier indicates the total number of available workspaces. To switch to a different workspace, you can click the identifier and select the workspace you want to use from the menu.

Switch to GNOME and from GNOME Classic

If you want to move from GNOME to GNOME Classic:

1. Then first save any open work, and then log out. You will get the logout option on the right side of the top bar and choose the correct option.

2. Click on Logout on a confirmation message prompt to confirm.

3. You will redirect to the login screen and enter your password in the entry box.

4. Click the icon displayed to the bottom left corner of the Sign In button, and select GNOME Classic.

5. Click the Sign In button. You will see the first UI of the GNOME Classic.

As above instruction you can change your any of the desktop environment.

Once you open the GNOME Classic as per instruction you will get the first window (see the following figure).

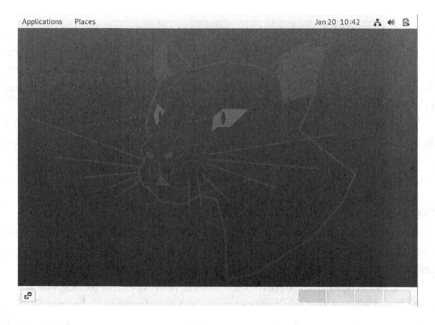

GNOME Classic desktop environment.

User Guide of GNOME Classic

The flashback uses the GNOME-panel package and a stack of older applets in GNOME Classic. The GNOME Classic version is pure GNOME Shell.

The whole retro-guide is created using a GNOME Shell extensions and also with silent tweaks. But together, they reshape the Shell to effectively resemble the "classic" Linux desktops of the past.

We are talking about some category-based application menu as shown in the following figure.

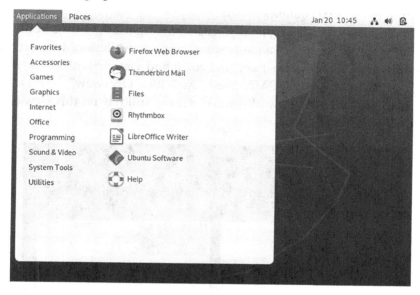

GNOME Classic Application menu.

A dedicated "Places" applet (see the following figure).

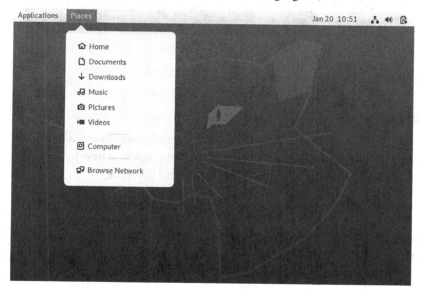

GNOME Classic Places menu.

The Button taskbar does not group the windows.

On-screen notifications nestle themselves in the upper right corner, like Ubuntu Notify OSD bubbles of old:

And a clock/calendar applet is placed on the right side of the screen.

But GNOME's Classic mode is something of an illusion. It scratches the surface or press the super key, and you'll find a few activities overview.

For instance, the GNOME Shell "Activities Overview" is present. Standard alt-tabbing and workspace switching still rely on this view (see the following figure).

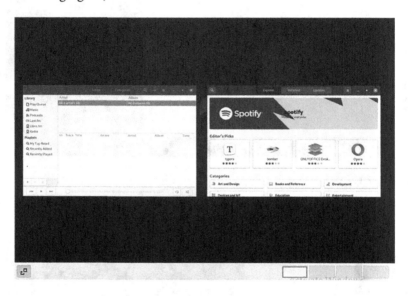

GNOME Classic Activities overview menu.

Enable GNOME Classic Mode on Ubuntu

You can easily install the GNOME Classic mode session on Ubuntu 18.04 LTS by installing a single package. Instead, pop opens a new terminal window (ctrl + t) and run the following command given below:

```
$ sudo apt install gnome-shell-extensions
```

Installation might take a few seconds. Then go ahead and log out of the current session and, from the login screen, click the cog icon and select "GNOME Classic" session. Log in as usual.

GNOME Classic has a GNOME Shell feature and mode for users who prefer a traditional desktop experience. GNOME Classic is based on

GNOME 3 technologies provides several changes to the user interface as given below.

You can see two options on the top bar, i.e., the Applications and Places menus.

First, the Applications menu is shown at the top left of the screen that gives the user access to applications organized into categories. The user can open the Activities Overview from that menu.

Second, the Places menu is shown next to the Applications menu on the top bar that gives them quick access to important folders, for example, Downloads or Pictures.

The taskbar is indicated at the bottom of the screen and features: a window list, a notification icon showed next to the window list, a short identifier for the currently active workspace and the total number of available workspaces shown next to the notification icon.

Following are the four available workspaces in GNOME Classic:

1. The number of workspaces available is by default set to 4.

2. Minimize and maximize buttons.

3. Window title bars in Classic feature the minimize and maximize buttons that allow the user to minimize the windows or maximize them to take up all of the space on the screen.

4. In GNOME Classic, you can use Super + Tab to switch windows.

The system menu is located on the top right corner. You can update some of your settings from this menu, find information about your Wi-Fi connection, switch users, log out, and turn off your computer.

The GNOME Classic Extensions

GNOME Classic is a set of GNOME Shell extensions. The GNOME Classic extensions are installed as dependencies of the GNOME-classic-session package, which provides components required to run a GNOME Classic session because the GNOME Classic extensions are enabled by default on Enterprise Linux 7. It is the default Red Hat Enterprise Linux 7 desktop user interface.

- AlternateTab (alternate-tab@gnome-shell-extensions.gcampax.github. com),

- Applications Menu (apps-menu@gnome-shell-extensions.gcampax. github.com),

- Launch new instance (launch-new-instance@gnome-shell-extensions. gcampax.github.com),

- Places Status Indicator (places-menu@gnome-shell-extensions.gcampax. github.com),

- Window List (window-list@gnome-shell-extensions.gcampax.github. com).

Switching from GNOME Classic to GNOME

The user can switch from Classic to GNOME by logging out. The cog-wheel opens a dropdown menu on the login screen containing GNOME Classic.

To switch from GNOME Classic to GNOME from within the user session, run the following command:

```
$ gnome-shell --mode=user -r &
```

To switch back to GNOME Classic from within the same user session, run the following command:

```
$ gnome-shell --mode=classic -r &
```

GNOME ON XORG

Xorg, commonly refer as simply X, is the most famous display server for Linux users. It has led to making it an ever-present requisite for GUI applications, resulting in massive adoption from most distributions.

GNOME on Xorg is precisely the same as GNOME but uses Xorg instead of Wayland. You might need this option if you use NVIDIA proprietary drivers or need to do things with Team viewer, OBS, or X forwarding over SSH. 4.

GNOME, the default run GNOME Shell on Wayland. Traditional X applications are run through Xwayland. Thus, it is a customized form of Shell rather than a distinct mode. GNOME on Xorg runs GNOME Shell using Xorg (see the following figure).

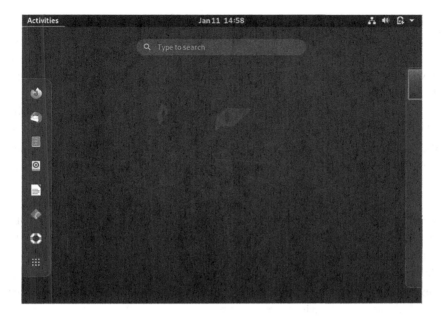

Desktop environment GNOME on Xorg interface.

UBUNTU ON WAYLAND

What Is Wayland?

The way to define Wayland is to call it a protocol used by window managers to communicate with the client and the C library of its protocol.

A compositing window manager colloquially is a windows manager that provides applications with an off-screen buffer for a separate window. A compositor can interact with the graphics and the window system creating:

- Transparency in windows

- Animations

- Drop shadows

The implemented by Wayland protocol can display servers running on the Kernel, X application, or a Wayland client such as rootless or full-screen X servers, other display servers, or basic applications.

The initial team of volunteer developers who helped develops the Wayland protocol created it as a more straightforward and faster replacement of X. X11 technology has been the default display server used by most Linux. Wayland handles applications in a standalone session of the protocol, and it improves performance because the server does not have to manage all applications at once. Instead, the required applications draw standalone items needed.

Wayland's development has improved, with more features like the XWayland that let users work with X11-based Wayland applications. Wayland specifies the communication between a display server and its clients. By default, the Ubuntu desktop does not start Wayland as it loads to the Xorg display server instead.

Whether GNOME uses X or Wayland should not affect a complete Linux distribution in a disruptive way. The Wayland libraries become GNOME dependencies and need to be available. The display manager knows how to launch a Wayland-based session in addition to establishing X-based sessions, and a few other plumbing components will have to learn about this new type of session. For GNOME, this part of the GNOME porting effort and 3rd party applications continue to work in GNOME via xwayland.

GNOME applications continue to work in X-based environments via the GTK + X backend.

How to Enable/Disable Wayland on Ubuntu

Assuming that GDM3 is your default display manager, edit the/etc/gdm3/custom.conf to disable or enable Wayland:

```
$ sudoedit /etc/gdm3/custom.conf
```

Restart your Ubuntu desktop using the below command:

```
$ sudo systemctl restart gdm3
```

To login to Ubuntu using the Wayland, click on the button and select Ubuntu on the Wayland option before you log in.

Wayland has features that are hard or impossible to support under Xorg:

- It has input transformation.

- Its transparent hardware overlays and direct rendering.

- It has isolating clients (like sandboxing) and makes it possible to reuse android drivers.

- per-crtc EGLSurfaces in Wayland means repainting and swapping only the monitor where content changes.

- It has a smooth transition between composited desktop and fullscreen clients (no X un redirect flicker).

- It liminates lag between the cursor and dragged windows (e.g., moving top levels or dnd icons).

- It has better remote display.

WHAT IS A GNOME SHELL EXTENSION?

A GNOME Shell Extension is a tiny piece of code that enhances the capability of the GNOME desktop.

You can install an add-on in the browser to disable ads. A third-party developer develops this add-on. Your web browser does not provide by default. Installing these add-ons enhances the capability of the web browser.

GNOME Shell Extensions are like third-party add-ons and plugins that you can install on GNOME. These extensions are created to perform specific display weather conditions, Internet speed, etc. Primarily, you can access them in the top panel.

There are GNOME Extensions that are not visible on the top panel. But they still tweak GNOME's behavior. For example, the middle mouse button can close an application with one such extension.

Installing GNOME Shell Extensions

Now you know what GNOME Shell Extensions are. Let's see how to install them using the following three ways you can use GNOME Extensions:

- Use a minimal set of extensions.

- Find and install extensions in the web browser.

- Download manually install extensions.

Before you learn to use GNOME Shell Extensions, you should install GNOME Tweak Tool in the Ubuntu distribution you are using. You can find it in the Software Center. Alternatively, you can use this command:

```
$ sudo apt install gnome-tweaks
```

You also need to know the version of Shell you are using. It helps determine whether an extension is compatible with your system or not. You can run the command below to find it:

```
$ gnome-shell - version
```

Method 1: Use GNOME-shell-extensions package. It is the easiest and safest way.

Ubuntu and other Linux distributions such as Fedora, provide a package with minimal GNOME extensions. You don't have to worry about compatibility as your Linux distribution tests it.

If you want a no-brainer, get this package, and you'll have 8–10 GNOME extensions installed.

```
$ sudo apt install gnome-shell-extensions
```

You'll have to reboot your system. When you start GNOME Tweaks, you will find a few extensions installed. You can toggle the button to start using an installed extension.

Method 2: Install GNOME Shell extensions from the browser.

GNOME project has an entire website to extensions. You can find, install, and manage extensions on this website. No need even for the GNOME Tweaks tool. Below is the GNOME Shell Extensions Website, https://extensions.gnome.org/. But to install extensions in a web browser, you need two things: a browser add-on and a native host connector in your system.

Step 1: Install a Browser Add-On
When you visit the Extensions website, you will see a message like this given below:

"To control GNOME Shell extensions using the site, you must install GNOME Shell integration that consists of two parts: a browser extension and native host messaging application."

You can click on the suggested add-on link by the web browser. You can install them from the link given:

- **For Google Chrome, Chromium, and Vivaldi:** Chrome web store use the link, https://chrome.google.com/webstore/detail/gnome-shell-integration/gphhapmejobijbbhgpjhcjognlahblep.

- **For Firefox:** Mozilla Add-ons use the link the, https://addons.mozilla.org/en-US/firefox/addon/gnome-shell-integration/

Step 2: Install Native Connector

Simply installing a browser add-on won't help you still. You will see an error like:

"Although GNOME Shell integration extension is running, native host connector is not detected in your system. Refer documentation for instructions about installing the connector."

How to install GNOME Shell Extensions?

The error came because you haven't installed the host connector yet. To do that, use this command:

```
$ sudo apt install chrome-gnome-shell
```

Step 3: Installing GNOME Shell Extensions in the Web Browser

Once you have completed these two requirements, you won't see any error message when you go to GNOME Shell Extension. It is a good idea to sort the extensions for the current version of GNOME.

A good thing to do is sort the extensions by GNOME Shell version. It is not mandatory. But happens here is that a developer creates an extension for the present GNOME version. Per year, there will be two more releases. But the developer did not have time to test or update their extension.

As a result, you would not know if that extension is compatible with your system or not. Despite being years old, the extension may work fine even in the newer GNOME Shell version.

- You can search for an extension to install a weather extension. Just search it and go for one of the search results.

- When you visit the page, you will see a toggle button.

- Click on it, and you will be prompted if you want to install this extension.

- Install here. Once installed, you will see that the toggle button is on and the setting option is available next. You can configure the extension via the setting option. You can disable the extension from here.

- You can configure the settings of an extension that has already been installed via the web browser in the GNOME Tweaks tool.

- You can see all installed extensions on the website under the already installed extensions section. You can also delete the extensions that you installed via the web browser.

- One major advantage of using the GNOME Extensions website is that you can see an update available for an extension.

Method 3: Install GNOME Shell Extensions manually.

It is not that you always have to install GNOME Shell extensions online. You can download the files and install them later, without needing the Internet.

- Go to the GNOME Extensions website download the extension with the latest version.

- Then, extract the downloaded file copy the folder to ~/.local/share/ gnome-shell/extensions directory. Go to the Home directory and press Crl + H to show hidden folders. To locate the .local folder here, and from there, you can find your path to the extensions directory.

- Once the files are copied in the directory, open the metadata.json file from inside it and look for the value of UUID.

- Make sure the name of the extension's folder is the same as the value of UUID in the metadata.json file. If not, rename the directory to the value of UUID.

- Almost there! Now restart GNOME Shell. Press Alt + F2 and enter r to continue GNOME Shell.

- Restart GNOME Tweaks too. You should see the manually installed GNOME extension in the Tweak tool. You can configure or enable the newly installed extension here.

It is pretty much all you need to know about installing GNOME Shell Extensions.

Remove GNOME Shell Extensions

Understandably, you might want to remove an installed GNOME Shell Extension.

If you installed it via a web browser, you can go to the installed extensions section on the GNOME website and remove it.

If you installed it manually, you could remove it by deleting the extension files from the ~/.local/share/gnome-shell/extensions directory.

CHAPTER SUMMARY

Ubuntu includes the GNOME desktop environment, which can be accessed during the installation or installed later using the tasksel command-line tool. Most other desktop environments like GNOME 3 are intended to provide a clean and easy-to-use windowing user interface. The critical areas of the GNOME desktop include the top bar, activities overview, and dash. In addition, GNOME supports various workspaces, keeping running applications organized and the screen clean. A variety of configuration options are available within the settings app, including desktop background settings, audio, network configuration, and Wi-Fi network selection.

CHAPTER 3

GNOME Applications

IN THIS CHAPTER

- ➤ Introduction of GNOME desktop environment
- ➤ gThumb application
- ➤ Corebird application
- ➤ GNOME Todo – Joplin
- ➤ GNOME Music – Rhythmbox
- ➤ FeedReader application
- ➤ Snappy application
- ➤ Epiphany browser application
- ➤ Vinagre remote desktop client application
- ➤ Gedit application
- ➤ Dia Diagram Editor application
- ➤ EasyTAG application
- ➤ GNOME Subtitles application
- ➤ And more

DOI: 10.1201/9781003311942-3

In Chapter 1, we have learned how to install the Gnome desktop environment on a computer running an Ubuntu Linux system. We use ways of installation such as command line or Ubuntu Software Application.

Here in this chapter, we have discussed the GNOME application and how it works, installed in your Ubuntu system, user interface guide, feature, and more. Again we will tell you what is GNOME as follow.

INTRODUCTION OF THE GNOME DESKTOP ENVIRONMENT

GNOME is a desktop environment – a graphical user interface that runs on top of a computer operating system – composed entirely of free software. It is a project that includes creating software development frameworks for the desktop and working on the programs which manage application launching, files handling, and window and task management. It used a pure GNOME 3 desktop environment with GNOME Shell rather than the Unity graphical shell. The GNOME desktop is one complete and accessible desktop environment in the Linux ecosystem, but the apps aren't preinstalled, so we need to download them.

It is the default experience in popular distributions like Fedora and Debian, and it's one of the primary options available in most others.

Regardless of which distribution you choose, the default applications tend to be the same when you fire up a GNOME desktop. You will likely see Firefox and LibreOffice alongside GNOME-specific applications like Gedit, Nautilus, Cheese, Calculator, Clocks, and Terminal.

There are many applications to choose from in distribution repositories. Nevertheless, only GNOME apps will have buttons in the window border and sufficiently use the application menu button at the top of the screen. Since some software is not labeled, new and seasoned Linux users alike can have a difficult time finding additional GNOME apps. Here's a list of several programs that did not come preinstalled with your distribution.

Here is a list of applications designed for use with the GNOME desktop environment.

GTHUMB APPLICATION

The gThumb is an open-source software image organizer, image viewer, and a well-integrated tool for GNOME desktop environments. Hence, it is also available for most of the Linux distros; Ubuntu comes with a default image viewer named as the eye of GNOME (or); this default app of Ubuntu has fundamental functionalities; on the other hand; gThumb acts as a multipurpose tool for image handlings in Ubuntu. It is the list of well-known tools of Ubuntu; this section is focused on gThumb we will guide you about the installation of this tool and the usage of gThumb in detail.

GNOME's default app for viewing images is Image Viewer and Eye of GNOME. But if you want to do more, look at any picture. You will need to find another app. You can edit images in GIMP, but that feels excessive for simple tasks like cropping and resizing.

gThumb is an image viewer that takes space somewhere between the two. A file manager in the sidebar lets you browse your machine without leaving the window. The edit button provides tools for adjusting the size of photos and altering the colors. gThumb can also organize photos into catalogs. Altogether, this makes gThumb a solid alternative to Picasa on Linux.

How to Install gThumb on Ubuntu

There are two ways to install the gThumb image viewer.

Install gThumb Using Ubuntu Software

Open the Software application and enter "gThumb" in the search bar. You will see the result in a while; click on the needed app as shown in the following figure.

gThumb Application icon.

The time you click on the Application; you can install it by clicking on the "Install" button as discussed below:

- When you click on this install button, the prompts window will come. It will ask for an authentication password: enter your user password and then enter.

- After the installation begins to start, the package will install in a few moments.

- Follow simple steps to confirm that the package is installed or not.

- Click on the "Applications" icon, which is on the taskbar of Ubuntu.

- Search "gThumb" and you will notice the application icon on your screen.

How to Install gThumb via the Terminal in Ubuntu

Open the terminal window by using the shortcut Alt + Ctrl + T; once it opens, execute the following command to install gThumb image viewer on your Ubuntu:

```
$ sudo apt Install gthumb
```

You will see the following output:

```
user@user-VirtualBox:~$ sudo apt Install gthumb
Reading package lists... Done
Building dependency tree...Done
Reading state information...Done
```

The following packages were installed and are no longer required:

```
caribou five-or-more four-in-a-row gir1.2-caribou-1.0
gir1.2-champlain-0.12
gir1.2-dazzle-1.0 gir1.2-gdata-0.0
gir1.2-geocodeglib-1.0
gir1.2-gfbgraph-0.2 gir1.2-grilo-0.3
gir1.2-gtkchamplain-0.12
gir1.2-mediaart-2.0 gir1.2-rest-0.7 gir1.2-tracker-2.0
gir1.2-zpj-0.0
gnome-chess gnome-clocks gnome-color-manager gnome-
core gnome-documents
```

Once it is installed, you need to open it by writing the name in the terminal and hitting enter, as shown below:

```
$ gthumb
```

How to Use gThumb on Ubuntu

This portion will provide a detailed discussion of the "gThumb" app to you. At first, open the Application by searching in "Application" of Ubuntu (see the following figure).

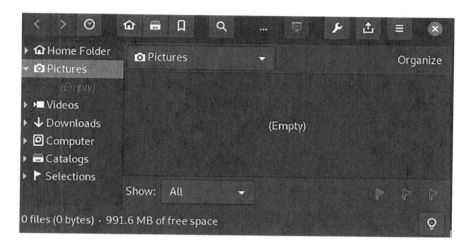

gThumb Application window.

Click on the icon to open it. By default, it is in the "Pictures" folder:

On the left column of the gThumb's application window, you can choose files to form available directories.

Click on any image in the "Pictures" directory; when you select an image, you will observe some options on the upper side of the window, as shown below:

You can perform the various actions from the menu bar.

You can navigate to full-screen mode just by clicking the first option as shown in the image below.

View the photo in actual size; fit the image according to the screen; customize the zoom settings.

You can rotate the image as per requirement.

Click on the information icon to get the brief information related to the selected image.

Once you clicked on the information icon, it will show you the related information on the right side of the window.

By selecting the option, you may also alter the image.

Using the edit option, you can simply adjust the colors, detailed rotation, and resize settings.

You can also add comments and tags to the image by using the option given below:

https://linuxhint.com/install-gthumb-ubuntu/

COREBIRD APPLICATION

It is an open-source Twitter client application. It works on any Linux distribution. You can manage your Twitter account with it. Its well-designed and nice-looking native Twitter client is perfect for you if you use Twitter regularly. It provides many features, mainly sharing images, tweeting, direct messages, following and unfollowing other accounts, searches, clickable hash tags, and much more.

Features

- Offers you to redesign the account wizard

- Offers save your media attachments very quickly

- Added "reply to multi-person tweet" features

- Text selection supports DM

The app is quick to load. Most of what you desire is accessible on the upper left-hand side. There you can browse through your newsfeed, view mentions, keep track of your favorites, keep up with direct messages, manage lists, add filters, and perform searches. You can change account settings and edit your profile. Getting to your profile page isn't as convenient as I'd like, but overall, this is one of the best ways to experience Twitter on an open-source desktop.

Users can install corebird via PPA or as Snap so that anyone can install it on all the Linux distros, which support Snap. There are many ways to install this app on Ubuntu or other Linux distros. Here I will be trying to give all those. You need to choose the right one for your system.

How to Install Corebird Snap on Ubuntu and Other Linux Distros

Open the Terminal Application and run the command to install this app as Snap-on Ubuntu or any snap supported Linux distros:

```
$ sudo snap install corebird
```

In Ubuntu, you have to install additional packages, which solve some while opening a link in Snap apps on a non-Snap browser. Now run the following command to install all essential packages given below:

```
$ sudo apt Install snapd-xdg-open
```

Install Corebird on Ubuntu via PPA

Suppose you want to use an essential way to install it via PPA.

Open the Terminal Window and type the commands one by one.

```
$ sudo add-apt-repository ppa:ubuntuhandbook1/corebird
$ sudo apt update
$ sudo apt Install corebird
```

Flatpak and Flathub

If you have set up Flatpak and Flathub on the system. This app can be installed from Flathub using the below command:

```
$ flatpak install flathub org.baedert.corebird
```

How to Uninstall

If you want to remove the apps, run the following command:

```
$ sudo snap remove corebird
```

For removing regular packages, use:

```
$ sudo apt remove --autoremove corebord
```

Avoid Snap installation if the Internet connection is slow because it requires more than 122 MB of data. In this case, follow the classic one – install Corebird via PPA, which will take only 2.2 MB of data.

GNOME TODO – JOPLIN

These days, many good options exist on the web or your phone, and you could easily do without a dedicated application for managing to-do lists. But we find that keeping work-related tasks consolidated to the place where we do my work – my computer – makes a bit of sense. We don't particularly need extensive tagging or other filtering methods through tasks. We say give me the basics, and GNOME Todo does precisely that.

It's more than just a simple.

For example, the app allows you assign different priorities to tasks, with colors displaying the list mode so that you can delineate between them.

You can choose to give due dates, add subtasks, and double-click on any to-do to add, edit or view detailed notes.

The app adheres to all of the standard GNOME app conventions, like header bar, single app menu, etc. It also integrates with GNOME Online Accounts to sync your tasks with a couple of online services.

We'd typically say something like, "you can learn more about the app on the GNOME Wiki," but, honestly, the wiki page tells you next to nothing. It could do with some information about the features, modes, plugins, screenshots showing the whole interface, etc.

Install and Use Joplin Note-Taking Application

You might know some across a point in life where you would have wanted to put your thoughts, your feelings, ideas, or a quote that you read somewhere which you came to like into words and preserve them or there might be an occasion where you came across some vital information at work and wanted to save it, and in these moments where note-taking applications come into play as they offer an easy and convenient way to store up information or data.

Now, as the digital revolution hit the shores of the world, technology came into existence, and that changed everything. Today, those parchments have converted into note-taking applications, which have made things so much easier and faster than earlier. However, finding an excellent note-taking application is quite the hassle as there are various tools and applications for taking notes.

The installation of such an app that goes by the name of Joplin has become very popular among the Linux community.

What Is Joplin?

Joplin is an open-source and free note-taking application bundled with many features. It is available for both desktops and mobile phones and even has a command-line version. Joplin is compelling and can handle the organization and management of notes categorized into multiple notebooks. It allows the searching of notes, adding tags to messages, and even importing and exporting files into several data-formats such as Evernote export, PDF, HTML, etc. It further allows users to synchronize their accounts to cloud services like Dropbox, OneDrive, etc., that back up its data and secure it. It has a web clipper for Firefox and Chrome, from which webpages can be saved as notes.

Installing Joplin

By using the following methods, we can install Joplin on Ubuntu.

Installing Joplin Using Snaps

It can easily install by using a snap version of it. Snaps are compressed packages containing the entire Application and all its dependencies inside of it. It is pretty helpful as now there is no hassle of separately installing the dependencies. To install Joplin from the Snapcraft, run the following command into the terminal.

```
user@user-VirtualBox:~$ sudo snap install joplin
joplin 2.3.2 from Marco Trevisan (Treviño) (3v1n0)
installed
```

Installing Joplin Using AppImage

Suppose you are not comfortable with the terminal. In that case, Joplin can also be installed through its AppImage, which is like the Application's executable file similar to what you see in Windows, and to download the AppImage, go to the official website of Joplin, and you can find it under the Desktop applications.

Go to that location where it was downloaded and right-click on it. Then, open the permissions tab and tick the checkbox next to Execute.

After this, double click on the AppImage file, and Joplin will run.

Installing Joplin Using Installer Script

Another method of installing Joplin is via the installer script, which establishes the latest version of Joplin directly from the GitHub repository. We have to run the update command so all the system cache is up-to-date, which can be done by running the following command in the terminal.

```
$ sudo apt-get update
```

To install Joplin, run the following command in the terminal:

```
$ wget -O - https://raw.githubusercontent.com/
laurent22/joplin/master/
Joplin_install_and_update.sh | bash
```

Using the Joplin

Joplin may find in the list of installed apps after it has been installed.

When you first launch this application, you will be welcomed by a user interface that is jam-packed with functionality. The interface features three panes, as seen in the image below: a sidebar with all of your notebooks displayed, a center bar with all of your notes inside that notebook, and a right pane with the Note Editor.

TODOIST APPLICATION

Install and Configure Todoist

The word Todoist is the short phonetic form of a To-Do List that can organize work, tasks and make quick notes. The Todoist can remember all of the works for you and recall you when you need them. If you work for different clients, it can also remind the high prioritized tasks.

Application is available for all Windows, Mac, iPhones, Linux, and Android systems. It allows set labels, filters on the worklist, and even customizes the Todoist theme based on work category.

Todoist on GNOME

Before, the Todoist tool was not available on GNOME. But there were many options to use the features through the third-party applications, but the official Todoist Application was available on GNOME. Then finally, Doist Inc has built the official Todoist tool for the Linux system. Can Installing the Todoist task manager tool on GNOME using the Snap and AppImage method.

It would help if you had the runtime Snap daemon installed on your system in the Snap method. And, for the AppImage method, we will see how you can install the Todoist tool by downloading the AppImage file. Now you will see how to install the Todoist tool on GNOME through Snap and AppImage methods.

Install Todoist on GNOME via Snap

The Snap daemon has popular, and users like the Snap store for the availability of many applications. Using this method to install the Todoist tool is a suitable method.

Here, we will see how to install the runtime daemon tool on various GNOME systems; later, we will go through the Todoist installation command on GNOME via Snap at the end of this method.

Installation

You can run the given command such as:

```
$ sudo snap install todolist
```

If you didn't get anything then visit the GNOME Software Application and search for Todo (see the following figure).

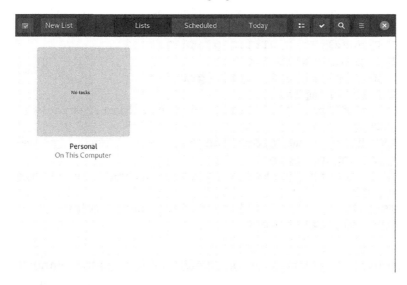

Todo List Application window.

GNOME MUSIC – RHYTHMBOX

Linux has a selection of music players, but only a couple integrates with the GNOME desktop environment. Right now, distributions tend to include Rhythmbox. An alternative is GNOME Music. Like most of the project's latest apps, don't expect much in the way of configuration. It is an app that can scan your music folder, displays albums in an attractive grid, and let you play tracks.

RHYTHMBOX APPLICATION

Install Rhythmbox

Install Rhythmbox by the following commands in the terminal:

```
$ sudo apt update
$ sudo apt install rhythmbox
```

```
user@user-VirtualBox:~$ sudo apt Install rhythmbox
Reading package lists...Done
Building dependency tree...Done
Reading state information...Done
```

The following packages were installed and are no longer required:

```
caribou five-or-more four-in-a-row girl.2-caribou-1.0
girl.2-champlain-0.12
girl.2-dazzle-1.0 girl.2-gdata-0.0
girl.2-geocodeglib-1.0
girl.2-gfbgraph-0.2 girl.2-grilo-0.3
girl.2-gtkchamplain-0.12
girl.2-mediaart-2.0 girl.2-rest-0.7 girl.2-tracker-2.0
girl.2-zpj-0.0
gnome-chess gnome-clocks gnome-color-manager gnome-
contacts gnome-core
gnome-documents gnome-games gnome-klotski gnome-maps
gnome-music
gnome-nibbles gnome-online-miners gnome-robots
gnome-shell-extensions
```

If you are looking for an open-source audio music player for Ubuntu flavors GNOME, then you are at the right place. There are many free music players available. Still, Rhythmbox stands out because of its stability, reliability, and ability to handle tens of thousands of songs and the support of plugins.

It is a GNOME-based music player, but it also integrates with other desktop environments. Some features of Rhythmbox are:

- It plays music from your local drive, stream Internet radio, and podcasts.

- It can make a smart playlist.

- It lets you enable gapless playback.

- Enables your audio CDs to be burned.

- It automatically searches artwork for the tracks.

- It allows SoundCloud integration.

- It displays lyrics if they are present in the database.

Rhythmbox is a default music player in many Linux distributions, including Ubuntu. It can be installed if it is not present in your distribution by default using a couple of methods. Let's check how to get the Latest Rhythmbox on your Ubuntu device.

Installing Rhythmbox on GNOME 3.36 and That 20.10 Using Ubuntu's Software Center

The method of installing a Rhythmbox audio player is less complex and accessible. Open the software store from the Application as shown in the following figure.

Then type Rhythmbox you will get the following result.

Now you can download it by clicking the "Install" button as shown in the following figure.

Once the downloading and installation are finished, the Rhythmbox app can now be viewed and open in applications. Now, Rhythmbox audio music player is ready to use.

Installing Rhythmbox Using the Terminal

In this method, the Rhythmbox application will be downloaded using the terminal and execute the below-mentioned command to download and install it:

```
$ sudo apt Install rhythmbox
```

While launching the Application you will see the window shown in the following figure.

Rythmbox Application window.

How to Uninstall Rhythmbox

If the player is installed using the software center application, to delete it, open the software center again and click on the "Installed." Find Rhythmbox and click remove.

Or by using command, run the following command:

```
$ sudo apt remove rhythmbox
```

Google Reader was over two years ago, and the RSS landscape has not been the same since. Several options have popped up, but none have quite the same reach. Still, if you prefer RSS to Reddit and want a decent dedicated client for your desktop, FeedReader is worth a look.

FEEDREADER APPLICATION

FeedReader is a modern GTK+ 3 client for online RSS services like tt-rss and others.

It currently supports Feedbin, Feedly, FreshRSS, InoReader, Local RSS, Nextcloud/ownCloud, The Old Reader, and Tiny Tiny RSS. It can combine all the advantages of web-based services like syncing across all your devices with everything you expect from a modern desktop application. It saves articles to read-it-later with Instapaper, Pocket, or Wallabag. Also, it shares articles with others via Email, Twitter, Telegram.

How to Install FeedReader

The software is available in Ubuntu 18.10, 19.04, and 19.10, but won't receive future updates.

To install the latest release in Ubuntu 18.04 and higher, open the terminal either via Ctrl + Alt + T or from the application menu, and run the following commands one by one:

First, you should run the command to install the flatpak framework:

```
$ sudo apt-get install flatpak
```

Add flathub repository, which hosts an extensive list of flatpak applications:

```
flatpak remote-add --if-not-exists flathub https:
//flathub.org/repo/flathub.flatpakrepo
```

or by snapd command

```
$ sudo snap install feedreader
```

The output will be:

```
user@user-VirtualBox:~$ sudo snap install feedreader
feedreader 0+git.9ac478f7 from Ken VanDine installed
```

Finally, install RSS client via command:

```
$ flatpak install flathub org.gnome.FeedReader
```

And future install updates if available via flatpak update org.gnome. FeedReader command.

Run the command in the terminal to remove FeedReader flatpak package:

```
$ flatpak uninstall org.gnome.FeedReader
```

Features

FeedReader Works With

- **Feedbin:** A fast, simple service that delivers a great reading experience.

- **Feedly:** One of the most popular online RSS services available.

- **FreshRSS:** A free, self-hostable aggregator. Probably the best, according to the developers.

- **InoReader:** Popular alternative to feedly with similar features.

- **Local RSS:** No online account or server needed. All data on your own hard drive.

- **Nextcloud:** Self hosted cloud that can do RSS and much, much more.

- **The Old Reader:** Welcome to the ultimate social RSS reader for The Open Web.

- **Tiny Tiny RSS:** Self hosted powerful but lightweight RSS reader.

Push to Read-It-Later

- **Instapaper:** It can save Anything. Read Anywhere.

- **Pocket:** The world's leading save-for-later service.

- **Wallabag:** It can save the web, freely.

Share with Others

- **Email:** It can share via email right from FeedReader.

- **Telegram:** It can share articles to your friends and groups easily from FeedReader.

- **Twitter:** Tweet about articles.

SNAPPY APPLICATION

It is an open-source media player that gathers the power and flexibility of gstreamer inside the comfort of a minimalistic clutter interface.

Enable snaps on Ubuntu and install snappy-m-o

Snaps are applications packaged with dependencies to run on all popular Linux distributions from a single build. They update automatically and roll back gracefully.

Snaps are installable from the Snap Store, an app store with an audience of millions.

Install snappy-m-o

Use the following command to install snappy-m-o:

```
$ sudo snap install snappy-m-o --edge –classic
```

Requirements

- Ubuntu Installed and Running

- Active Internet Connection to download Brasero

- Sudo Privileges

Features of Brasero

- Able to support various backends: cdrtools, growisofs, and libburn

- Can be used for the editing of discs' contents

- Automatic filtering for unwanted files

- Multisession and Joliet extension support

- Writing the image to the hard drive

- Checking disc file integrity

- Write CD-TEXT information

- Search for audio files inside dropped folders

- The full edition of silences between tracks

- Can copy a CD/DVD to the hard drive

- Erase CD/DVD (for Rewritable CD/DVDs)

- Project saving and loading

- Burning CD/DVD images and cue files

- Song, image, and video previewer

- Device detection and File change notification

- Customizable GUI (when used with GDL)

- Supports Drag & Drop/Cut & Paste from files

How to Install Brasero on Ubuntu?

You can install Brasero by two methods:

- Graphical method

- Using terminal

First, let's start with the visual way.
Install Brasero on Ubuntu graphically.
Brasero is available in the Ubuntu software center:

- Start the Ubuntu Software Center.

- Search for Brasero. Click on the result.

- Click on Install and provide authentication to install the Brasero.

- Once installation is finished, you'll see the option to remove.

- Start Brasero via the applications menu.

Install Brasero on Ubuntu via Terminal

Brasero is available in the Ubuntu repository to install it easily using the apt command.

Before installing Brasero, it's recommended to update the software repositories.

```
$ sudo apt update
```

Now, to install Brasero, run:

```
$ sudo apt Install brasero
```

Once installation is finished, you can start Brasero using the command:

```
$ brasero
```

You will get the window as shown in the following figure.

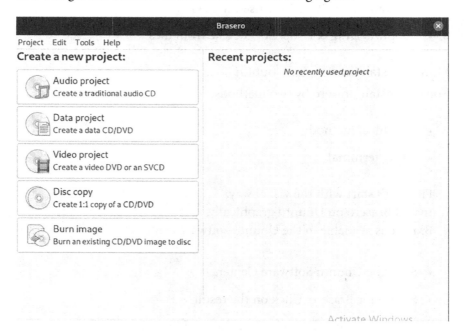

Brasero Application window.

To Uninstall Brasero from Ubuntu

If you want to remove Brasero, then you can do so from Ubuntu Software Center or execute the below command using the terminal:

```
$ sudo apt remove brasero
```

EPIPHANY BROWSER APPLICATION

To Install Epiphany Browser in Ubuntu

It is an open-source web browser for the GNOME desktop environment and provides a simple and easy-to-use Internet browsing experience. It supports plugins that enhance its default functionality. The installation of the Epiphany browser in Ubuntu GNOME is explained in this section.

Installation of Epiphany Browser

First, add the required repository with the following command.

```
user@user-VirtualBox:~$ sudo add-apt-repository
ppa:gnome3-team/gnome3
```

[sudo] password for user:

Before upgrading system to a new Ubuntu release from 16.04 to 16.10, you need to run "ppa-purge ppa:gnome3-team/gnome3" first.

*** You should run "sudo apt-get dist-upgrade" to avoid the problems. ***

Please study the results before pressing "Y" to ensure that no packages are deleted.

=== Bugs ===

To report issues against packages in this PPA, please use the "ubuntu-bug" command.

=== End of Life ===

This PPA is no longer maintained for Ubuntu 18.04 LTS versions. Please ppa-purge this PPA and consider updating to a newer Ubuntu version if you are running an older edition.

Updates will only be available in this PPA for 7 months from the initial release of the related Ubuntu series, unless otherwise stated.

https://lists.ubuntu.com/archives/ubuntu-gnome/2017-March/004229.html

More info: https://launchpad.net/~gnome3-team/+archive/ubuntu/gnome3

. . . .

To update the added repository with "apt-get update" command. Update the added repository with "apt-get update" command.

```
user@user-VirtualBox:~$ sudo apt-get update
Hit:1 http://in.archive.ubuntu.com/ubuntu focal
InRelease
Hit:2 http://in.archive.ubuntu.com/ubuntu focal-
updates InRelease
Hit:3 http://in.archive.ubuntu.com/ubuntu focal-
backports InRelease
Hit:4 http://security.ubuntu.com/ubuntu focal-security
InRelease
Ign:5 http://ppa.launchpad.net/gnome3-team/gnome3/
ubuntu focal InRelease
Ign:6 http://ppa.launchpad.net/snappy-dev/beta/ubuntu
focal InRelease
Err:7 http://ppa.launchpad.net/gnome3-team/gnome3/
ubuntu focal Release
404 Not Found [IP: 91.189.95.85 80]
```
. . . .

To install epiphany package with the below given command:

```
user@user-VirtualBox:~$ sudo apt-get install
epiphany-browser
Reading package lists... Done
Building dependency tree. . Done
Reading state information... Done
```

The following packages were installed and are no longer required:

```
caribou five-or-more four-in-a-row girl.2-caribou-1.0
girl.2-champlain-0.12
girl.2-dazzle-1.0 girl.2-gdata-0.0
girl.2-geocodeglib-1.0
girl.2-gfbgraph-0.2 girl.2-grilo-0.3
girl.2-gtkchamplain-0.12
```

```
girl.2-mediaart-2.0 girl.2-rest-0.7 girl.2-tracker-2.0
girl.2-zpj-0.0
gnome-chess gnome-clocks gnome-color-manager gnome-
contacts gnome-core
gnome-documents gnome-games gnome-klotski gnome-maps
gnome-music
gnome-nibbles gnome-online-miners gnome-robots
gnome-shell-extensions
.  .  .  .  .
```

Another way to install epiphany is snapd, which is as follows:

```
$ sudo snap install epiphany
```

The output will be as shown in the following figure.

Epiphany Application window.

Features:

1. Reader Mode Improvements
   There was a lot of noise over Epiphany's reader mode when added last year. The clutter-reduction feature is set to get even better in Epiphany 3.3.
   There is a keyboard shortcut to toggle reader mode on and off. When you start a page that could do with a quick prune, tap Super + Shift + R to dial things back, and critical combo saves you from having to hunt and peck in menus or remember which toolbar button is which.

Then, a small set of preferences for reader mode have added. These let improve the styling and look of reader mode pages. You can choose between light and dark pages and between a sans or serif font.

2. Native PDF Viewing
Epiphany supports viewing PDFs in the browser using the libevince library.

It will be handy if you read a lot of PDFs online. Now, Epiphany will download a PDF when you click on a link to a PDF file, requiring you to open it in a separate app, like Evince or Okular.

But it is hoped that for its next release, the PDF will open in the same tab allowing you to read, scan, and pan around the document without any awkward shunting to another app.

3. Additional Zoom Steps
Epiphany page zoom, using the buttons or keyboard shortcuts, jumps up from 100% to 125% to 150%, and similarly down to 75% to 50%.

4. More Tab Options
Extra tab options feature in the new builds of Epiphany, including:

- It reloads all tabs

- Can reload individual tab

- It reopens the last closed tab

- Can close all other tabs

Extra, the new tab button has move to the left-hand side of the header bar, where now it stays. Also, middle-clicking the homepage button will open your homepage in a new tab. No, these are not head-spinning changes, but they are worth a shout-out nonetheless.

VINAGRE REMOTE DESKTOP CLIENT APPLICATION

It is a remote desktop client created by the GNOME project. It supports various remote desktop protocols and supports the following remote desktop protocols given below.

- VNC – stands for Virtual Network Computing

- RDP – stands for Remote Desktop Protocol

- SPICE – stands for Simple Protocol for Independent Computing Environments

- SSH – stands for Secure Shell

You can connect to your remote computer using multiple remote desktop protocols using the Vinagre remote desktop client.

This section will show you how to install the Vinagre remote desktop client on some popular Linux distributions. So, let's get started.

Install Vinagre

It is available in the repository of Ubuntu. So, you can also install the Vinagre remote desktop client on Ubuntu operating system.

First, update the APT repository cache with the following command:

```
$ sudo apt update
```

To install the Vinagre remote desktop on Ubuntu, run the following command:

```
$ sudo apt Install vinagre
```

To confirm the installation, then press Y and then press <Enter>.

All the required packages are being installed. It takes a while to complete and opens Vinagre remote desktop client opens (see the following figure).

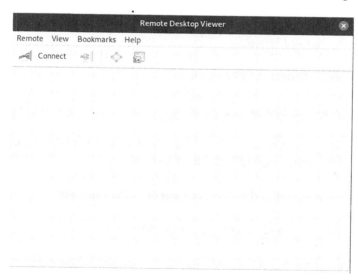

Vinagre Application window.

GEDIT APPLICATION

Gedit is a powerful word processor and code editor part of GNOME. Ubuntu uses GNOME as its desktop environment. Therefore, it has been installed by default at the beginning of the Canonical distribution.

One of the features of Gedit is that having the typical word processor functions, such as copy, paste, print, spell checker, it has the option of developing programming files in several languages. It has syntax highlighting for multiple programming languages, idealizing a small edition or visualizing the code. It is open source and compatible with the Linux universe.

Install the latest version of Gedit on the GNOME desktop environment.

Gedit is installed and included in Ubuntu installation as part of GNOME. So we do not have to do anything to install it.

To uninstall the Gedit package that includes Ubuntu.

So, open a terminal and run:

```
$ sudo apt remove gedit
```

If you would like to install an updated version of Flatpak PPA.

```
$ sudo add-apt-repository ppa:alexlarsson/flatpak
$ sudo apt update
```

And finally, install Flatpak:

```
$ sudo apt Install Flatpak
```

Gedit is hosted on Flathub, so we must add this repository to Flatpak.

```
$ flatpak remote-add - if-not-exists flathub https:
//flathub.org/repo/flathub.flatpakrepo
```

And now we can install the latest version of Gedit running:

```
$ flatpak install flathub org.gnome.gedit
```

So, you can run it from the main menu or with the following command:

```
flatpak run org.gnome.gedit
```

Removing Gedit

If you want to remove Gedit from your system, there is no major trick. To do same, open a terminal window and execute the following command:

```
$ flatpak uninstall - user org.gnome.gedit
```

And with that, the whole installation process will start.

If you want, you can also uninstall Flatpak, but this is optional. To do so, you only have to execute the following command.

```
$ sudo apt autoremove Flatpak
```

Another method to install gedit is given below:

```
$ sudo apt Install gedit
```

Now this Application using

```
$ gedit
```

The output will be, as shown in the following figure.

Gedit Application window.

Gedit Text Editor Features

- **Insert Current Date and time:** Inserting a date and time is a super handy feature with just a click. It is often needed when maintaining a log as a simple text file. Now, put the cursor where you would like to insert date and time, then from the menu, click Tools > Insert Date and Time. Use your date and time format in the following dialog and click Insert.

- **Enable Auto-save options and Create Auto Backup:** This editor has two important features, which are turned off by default. They are auto save and auto backup. Go to Menu > Preferences > Editor > File Saving. It enables the Create a backup and Autosave files options. The gedit can save the file automatically, and you don't need to worry about losing your data.

- **Top Keyboard Shortcuts:** Keyboard shortcuts are handy for productivity come with many Keybaord shortcuts apart from the traditional method. You can find in Menu > Keyboard shortcuts. For example, you can convert letters to uppercase or lower case using CTRL + U and CTRL + L. Many features you can find in the below dialog.

- **Themes:** The gedit comes with predefined color schemes for the editor window. You can change the editor's background, font style, text color, and find them in the menu > preferences > Font, and Colors.

- **Split Window and Tab Grouping:** Open various tabs using CTRL + T or open multiple documents. Then press ALT + CTRL + N. It would be best to get a split-screen with a separator for any opened tabs. Now you can work on various documents side by side without leaving gedit.
  You can create more split windows to organize file tabs by pressing the ALT + CTRL + N multiple times. And you can drag the tabs to separate groups for arrangements.

- **Highlight Incorrect Spellings:** You can highlight the incorrect words and spell check using the Spell Checker plugin. To do so, go to Menu > Preferences > Plugins and check the Spell Checker plugin. Now to do a spell check for your document, press SHIFT + F7. It will bring up the spell check dialog.

Dash to Dock on GNOME Shell Extension

There are many themes, icons, extensions, and cursors to customize the desktop appearance then Dash to Dock is one of them.

It is an extension for the GNOME 3 environment that allows the various adjusting settings related to the Dock. It modifies the default Ubuntu dock to macOS-styled Dock, which ultimately helps launch and switch applications quickly and conveniently.

How to Install Dash to Dock

GNOME Tweak Tool is required in order to install Dash to Dock. If you don't already have it, use the following command to obtain it:

```
$ sudo apt Install gnome-tweak-tool
```

If you get the "Package not found" problem, use the command following to add the "universe" repository:

```
$ sudo add-apt-repository universe
```

It's time to download the Dash to Dock extension after successfully downloading the GNOME Tweak Tool.

To install Dash to Dock, go to the following URL in your browser: https://extensions.gnome.org/extension/

It asks you to install the browser extension first, which you should do by clicking and installing it.

Following installation, you will be asked with "Permissions," as seen below. Click the "Add" button to proceed.

The extension will install, and the icon will display in the browser window's upper right corner.

Then search "Dash to Dock" extension and click on the button to turn it "On," and now, launch the "GNOME Tweak Tool," go to the "Extensions" tab and enable it.

Position and Size

The option you will see is "Position and Size." There are several settings like:

- The positioning of the Dock
- Dock size limit

- Icon size limit

- Auto hiding dock

Launchers

The "Launchers" tab is the next tab. This area contains information on window previews, workspaces, and monitors. The "Applications" icon may be moved to the left or right as needed, or it can be removed entirely. Trash cans can also be enabled or disabled.

Behavior

In the tab, you can assign shortcut keys to the applications. Then, you can assign functions upon "Click Action" and "Scroll Action."

Appearance

It is all about modifying the dock's appearance and changing the theme; you can assign a default theme or customize some dock options separately.

Reduce the gap between apps by shrinking the dash.

Indicators for the Windows counter: Active or open applications can be identified by a variety of signs. Dots, squares, segments, solids, and other shapes are examples.

- **Dash Color:** It allows you to modify the dash's color, which is now black.

- **Opacity:** It changes the dash's opacity.

  - **Straight the corner:** The dash corners are round by default, but by selecting this option, you may make them obvious.

DIA DIAGRAM EDITOR APPLICATION

After updating the Packages now, we are ready to install the Dia Diagram Editor application. For that, we do not have to install any 3rd party PPA repository as it's a part of the default repository of Ubuntu. So let's go and install the Dia Diagram Editor package using the below command.

To update the added repository with "apt-get update" command.

Update the added repository with "apt-get update" command.

```
user@user-VirtualBox:~$ sudo apt-get update
Hit:1 http://in.archive.ubuntu.com/ubuntu focal
InRelease
```

```
Hit:2 http://in.archive.ubuntu.com/ubuntu focal-
updates InRelease
Hit:3 http://in.archive.ubuntu.com/ubuntu focal-
backports InRelease
Hit:4 http://security.ubuntu.com/ubuntu focal-security
InRelease
Ign:5 http://ppa.launchpad.net/gnome3-team/gnome3/
ubuntu focal InRelease
Ign:6 http://ppa.launchpad.net/snappy-dev/beta/ubuntu
focal InRelease
Err:7 http://ppa.launchpad.net/gnome3-team/gnome3/
ubuntu focal Release
404 Not Found [IP: 91.189.95.85 80]
........
```

After updating the Packages now, we are ready to install the Dia Diagram Editor application. For that, we do not have to install any third-party PPA repository as it's a part of the default repository of Ubuntu. So let's go and install the Dia Diagram Editor package using the below command.

```
user@user-VirtualBox:~$ sudo apt-get install dia
```

[sudo] password for user:

```
Reading package lists... Done
Building dependency tree... Done
Reading state information... Done
```

The following packages were installed and are no longer required:

```
caribou five-or-more four-in-a-row girl.2-caribou-1.0
girl.2-champlain-0.12
girl.2-dazzle-1.0 girl.2-gdata-0.0
girl.2-geocodeglib-1.0
girl.2-gfbgraph-0.2 girl.2-grilo-0.3
girl.2-gtkchamplain-0.12
girl.2-mediaart-2.0 girl.2-rest-0.7 girl.2-tracker-2.0
girl.2-zpj-0.0
gnome-chess gnome-clocks gnome-color-manager gnome-
contacts gnome-core
gnome-documents gnome-games gnome-klotski gnome-maps
gnome-music
```

```
gnome-nibbles gnome-online-miners gnome-robots
gnome-shell-extensions
```

We have installed the Dia Diagram Editor package, as you can see above. Now to confirm the same, use the below command.

```
$ sudo dpkg -1 dia
```

Now enter the dia command at the shell to open the application command given below.

```
$ dia
```

We have opened the Dia Diagram Editor Application with the above command, and you can also open the Dia Diagram Editor Application graphically using Search your Ubuntu Desktop Application box (see the following figure).

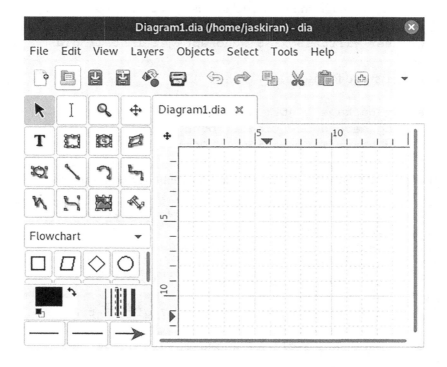

Dia Application window.

To Uninstall Dia Diagram Editor

If you don't like Dia Diagram Editor Application and want to uninstall the Application from your system

```
$ sudo dpkg -r dia-shapes
```

EASYTAG APPLICATION

It is a simple application for viewing and editing tags in audio files.

It supports various files, such as MP3, MP2, MP4/AAC, FLAC, Ogg Opus, Ogg Speex, Ogg Vorbis, MusePack, Monkey's Audio, and WavPack files, which work under Linux or Windows.

Features

It is used to view, edit, write tags of MP3, MP2 files (using ID3 tag with pictures), FLAC files (using FLAC Vorbis tag), Ogg Opus files (using Ogg Vorbis tag), Ogg Speex (using Ogg Vorbis tag), Ogg Vorbis files (using Ogg Vorbis tag), MP4/AAC (using MP4/AAC tag), MusePack, Monkey's Audio, and WavPack files (using the APE tag).

- **It can edit more tag fields:** title, artist, album, disc number, year, track number, comment, composer, original artist/performer, copyright, URL, encoder name, and attached picture.

- **Auto-tagging:** filename and directory to complete the fields automatically

- It may rename files and folders directly from the tag or by loading a text file

- It can process selected files of the selected directory

- It has the ability to browse subdirectories

- It has a playlist generator window

- It supports recursion for tagging, removing, renaming, saving

- It can set a field (artist, title) to all other files

- It reads and displays file header information (bitrate, time)

- Auto-completion of the date if a partial one is entered

- Undo and redo last changes

- Supports straightforward and explicit interface

- Ability to process tag and file name that convert letters into upper-case, lowercase

- It has the ability to open a directory or a file with an external program

- It supports CDDB using Freedb.org and Gnudb.org servers (manual and automatic search)

- A tree-based browser or a view by artist and album

- A list to select files

- A file searching window

- It can translate into many languages

- It is written in C and uses GTK+ for the GUI

- Packages available for Linux and Windows

- Ability to use an external program to open a directory or a file

- A tree-based browser

- A list to select files

- A file searching window

Installing EasyTAG

Install easytag by entering the following commands in the terminal:

```
$ sudo apt update
user@user-VirtualBox:~$ sudo apt-get update
Hit:1 http://in.archive.ubuntu.com/ubuntu focal
InRelease
Hit:2 http://in.archive.ubuntu.com/ubuntu focal-
updates InRelease
Hit:3 http://in.archive.ubuntu.com/ubuntu focal-
backports InRelease
```

```
Hit:4 http://security.ubuntu.com/ubuntu focal-security
InRelease
Ign:5 http://ppa.launchpad.net/gnome3-team/gnome3/
ubuntu focal InRelease
Ign:6 http://ppa.launchpad.net/snappy-dev/beta/ubuntu
focal InRelease
Err:7 http://ppa.launchpad.net/gnome3-team/gnome3/
ubuntu focal Release
404 Not Found [IP: 91.189.95.85 80]
........
```

After updating,

```
$ sudo apt Install easytag
```

```
user@user-VirtualBox:~$ sudo apt Install easytag
```

[sudo] password for user:

```
Reading package lists... Done
Building dependency tree... Done
Reading state information... Done
```

The following packages were preinstalled and are no longer required:

```
caribou five-or-more four-in-a-row gir1.2-caribou-1.0
gir1.2-champlain-0.12
gir1.2-dazzle-1.0 gir1.2-gdata-0.0
gir1.2-geocodeglib-1.0
gir1.2-gfbgraph-0.2 gir1.2-grilo-0.3
gir1.2-gtkchamplain-0.12
gir1.2-mediaart-2.0 gir1.2-rest-0.7 gir1.2-tracker-2.0
gir1.2-zpj-0.0
gnome-chess gnome-clocks gnome-color-manager gnome-
contacts gnome-core
gnome-documents gnome-games gnome-klotski gnome-maps
gnome-music
gnome-nibbles gnome-online-miners gnome-robots
gnome-shell-extensions
```

When you open Application the output will be, as shown in the following figure.

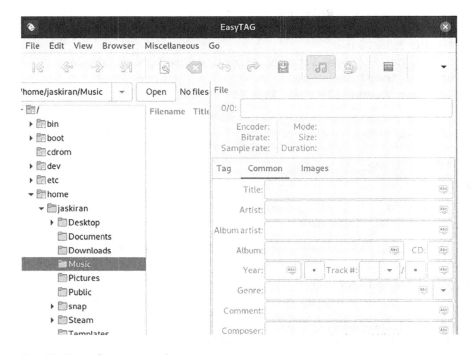

EasyTAG Application window.

GNOME SUBTITLES APPLICATION

It is an open-source and free subtitle editor for Linux without using a heavy video editor app. It allows you to add subtitles and captions to your video with preview, timing synchronization, translation, spell-checking support, and more.

GNOME Subtitles are written in C# and released under the GNU General Public License (GPL) version 2 or later.

GNOME Subtitles features are:

- subtitle editing

- translation

- synchronization and

- supports the most common text-based subtitle formats.

Other changes are:

- Rewrite GStreamer media playback engine.

- Fix audio and video playback issues.

- Update AppData and Desktop files.

- Subtitle lines displayed on video are now refreshed immediately if changed.

- And various bug fixes.

Install Gnome Subtitles

Add Ubuntu PPA in GNOME.

The software developer maintains an Ubuntu PPA containing the latest Ubuntu 16.04, Ubuntu version 18.04, 20.04, and 21.10.

Press Ctrl + Alt + T on the keyboard to open the terminal. Then execute the command below to add the PPA:

```
sudo add-apt-repository ppa:pedrocastro/ppa
```

Type user password when it asks and hit Enter to continue.

To Update or Install GNOME Subtitles

After adding the PPA, you may run the command below one by one to install the software package:

```
$ sudo apt update
$ sudo apt Install gnome-subtitles
```

Or update the package via "Software Updater" if an old version is present in your system.

To Remove GNOME Subtitles and PPA

Press Ctrl + Alt + T the keyboard shortcut to open the terminal, to remove the PPA, and run the command:

```
$ sudo add-apt-repository --remove ppa:pedrocastro/ppa
```

And remove the subtitle editor via command:

```
$ sudo apt remove --autoremove gnome-subtitles
```

EYE OF GNOME APPLICATION

It is the official default image viewer for the GNOME desktop environment, also known as Image Viewer. Another official image viewer for GNOME, also called gThumb, has more advanced features like image organizing and image editing functions.

GNOME's Eye provides primary effects for improved viewings such as zooming, full-screen, rotation, and transparent image background control. It has many official plug-ins to extend its features or change its behavior.

File Formats

It supports the following file formats:

RAS (Sun Raster), SVG (Scalable Vector Graphics), TGA (Truevision Targa), TIFF (Tagged Image File Format), WBMP (Wireless Application Protocol Bitmap Format), XBM (X BitMap), XPM (X PixMap), ANI (Animation), BMP (Windows Bitmap), GIF (Graphics Interchange Format), ICO (Windows Icon) JPEG (Joint Photographic Experts Group), PCX (PC Paintbrush), PNG (Portable Network Graphics), PNM (Portable Any map from the PPM Toolkit).

Limitations

It does not support WebP, DirectDraw Surface (.dds), or JPEG 2000, but gThumb, another official GNOME image viewer, has supported WebP since September 2012.

Install Eye of GNOME

Eye of GNOME is available through the Bionic Main repository. It can easily install through the command line using the apt-get command.

Open your Terminal application either through the system Application You can launcher Search or the Ctrl + Alt + T shortcut.

The next step is to update your system's repository index through the following command:

```
$ sudo apt-get update
```

It helps you install the latest available version of the software from the Internet. Note that only an authorized user can add, remove, and configure software on Ubuntu.

Now you are ready to install imgViewer; you can do by running the following command as sudo:

```
$ sudo apt-get install eog
```

The system may ask you the password for sudo and provide you with a Y/n option to continue the installation then enter Y and then hit enter; the software will install on your system. However, the process can take some time, depending on your Internet speed.

Run the Application with $eog command,

The output will be, as shown in the following figure.

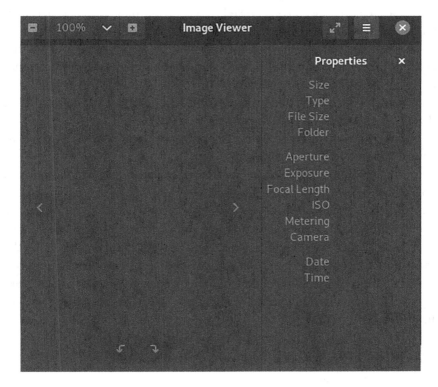

Eye of GNOME Application window.

You can check the version number of the Application and also verify that it is indeed installed on your system through the following command:

```
$ eog -version
```

The output will be as shown in the previous figure.

Launch and Use Eye of GNOME

You can launch the Application by entering the keywords "image viewer" in the Launcher Search bar, as follows:

You can also use the following command in the Terminal to launch the Application:

```
$ eog &
```

You can use the settings to open an image by browsing for it.

Eye of GNOME is the default image viewer for GNOME. Therefore, whenever you open an image, it will open in the Image Viewer/EOG. If it is not set as default viewer, you can right-click on an image, select Open with Other Application, and select Image Viewer from the list of applications.

You can set Image Viewer as the default photo viewing tool via the Settings utility. The easiest way to do is to search for "default applications" in the Application Launcher Search.

When you open the listed result entry, it will open the Settings utility in the Details > Default Applications view as follows:

N the Photos drop-down, select Image Viewer, and it will now be set as your default photo viewing tool.

With this lightweight, secure, and readily available image viewer, you do not need to search for anything else.

Hitori is a small application written to play the eponymous puzzle game, which is similar in theme to more popular puzzles such as Sudoku.

It depends on GTK+ 3 and Cairo 1.4 and has full support for playing the game (i.e., it checks all three rules are satisfied). It has undo/redo support, can give hints, and allows for cells to be tagged with one of two different tags to aid in solving the puzzle. It has support for anything from 5 × 5 to 10 × 10 grids.

HITORI APPLICATION

Installation of Hitori

Now, you need to update your system with the command:

```
$ sudo apt-get update
```

The above command will download the package lists for the GNOME desktop environment on your system. It will update the list of the newest versions of packages and their dependencies on your system.

After downloading the latest package list with the help of the above, you can run the installation process.

Installing hitori:

After the update, use the subsequent command to install hitori:

```
$ sudo apt-get install hitori
```

The above command confirm before installing the package on your Ubuntu Operating System. If you are not logged in, the installer will ask you for the root password. After completing the installation, you can use the package on your system.

Run the Application using the below command:

```
$ hitori
```

The output will be as shown in the following figure.

Hitori Application window.

To uninstall or remove hitori:

The commands for uninstalling the hitori from Ubuntu GNOME. You can easily use the apt control and remove the package from Linux Operating System for uninstalling this package.

To remove the hitori following command is used:

```
$ sudo apt-get remove
hitori
```

The following command is used to remove the hitori package along with its dependencies:

```
$ sudo apt-get remove --auto-remove hitori
```

It will remove hitori and its dependent packages, which are no longer needed in the system.

Completely removing Hitori using all configuration files:

The following command should be used with care as it deletes all the configuration files and data:

```
$ sudo apt-get purge hitori
```

or you can use the following command also:

```
$ sudo apt-get purge --auto-remove hitori.
```

GNOME-MINES APPLICATION

Install GNOME-mines

First, update your system using the command:

```
$ sudo apt-get update
```

The above command will download the package lists for Ubuntu 17.04 on your system. It will update the list of the newest versions of packages and their dependencies on your system.

After downloading the latest package list with the help of the above, you can run the installation process.

```
$ sudo apt-get install gnome-mines
```

The output will be as shown in the following figure.

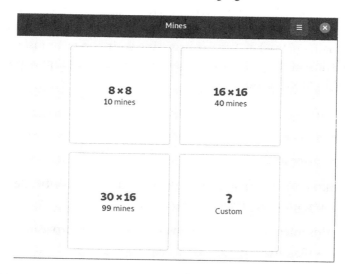

GNOME-mines Application window.

If GNOME-mines is not installed on your computer, the command "dpkg -L GNOME-mines" will be the following error.

To uninstall or remove GNOME-mines:

Here are the commands for uninstalling the GNOME-mines from Ubuntu GNOME. You can easily use the apt control and remove the package from Linux Operating System for uninstalling this package.

To remove the GNOME-mines following command is used:

```
$ sudo apt-get remove
GNOME-mines
```

The following command is used to remove the GNOME-mines package along with its dependencies:

```
$ sudo apt-get remove --auto-remove gnome-mines
```

This will remove GNOME-mines and all their dependent packages, which are no longer needed in the system.

POSTR APPLICATION

Postr is an uploading tool for GNOME, which aims to be simple to use but exposing enough of Flickr to be helpful. It uploads photos to Flickr Postr is a Flickr uploading tool for the GNOME desktop, which aims to be simple to use but exposing enough of Flickr to be useful. It has a simple user inter-face, and lets you set common attributes for your photos: title, description, tags, sets, groups, privacy, licence, etc. It is integrated with Nautilus: you can either run postr when you are browsing your photos or just drag them from Nautilus to drop them in Postr. Homepage: http://projects.gnome.org/postr/ Python-Version: 2.6

Features

- Simple user interface

- Set the common attributes for your photos such as title, description, tags, sets, groups, privacy, license, etc.

- Nautilus integration can run postr when you are browsing your photos by dragging.

- Session management, you can save your session and continue working on it later.

Quick Installation of postr

First, update your system with the command:

```
$ sudo apt-get update
```

After updating the OS, run the following command to install the package:

```
$ sudo apt-get install postr
```

The above command is confirmed before installing the Ubuntu GNOME Operating System package. If you are not logged in as su, the installer will ask you for the root password. After completing the installation, you can use the package on your system.

To Uninstall or Remove postr

Now the commands for uninstalling the postr from Ubuntu. You can eas-ily use the apt command and remove the package from system for unin-stalling this package.

To remove the postr following command is used:

```
$ sudo apt-get remove postr
```

The following command is used to remove the postr package along with its dependencies:

```
$ sudo apt-get remove --auto-remove postr
```

This will remove postr and all its dependent packages which is no longer needed in the system.

Completely removing postr with all configuration files:

The following command should be used with care as it deletes all the configuration files and data:

```
$ sudo apt-get purge postr
```

or you can use the following command also:

```
$ sudo apt-get purge --auto-remove postr
```

GNOME-TAQUIN APPLICATION

It is a computer version of the 15-puzzle and other sliding puzzles. The object is to move tiles to reach their places, either indicated with numbers or with parts of a great image.

Quick Installation of GNOME-taquin

To update command to the package repositories and get the latest package information to execute the following command:

```
$ sudo apt-get update -y
```

To install the taquin run the command with the -y flag to quickly install the packages and dependencies.

```
$ sudo apt-get install -y gnome-taquin
```

Completely removing GNOME-taquin with all configuration files:

The following command should use with care as it deletes all the configuration files and data:

```
$ sudo apt-get purge gnome-taquin
```

or you can use the following command also:

```
$ sudo apt-get purge --auto-remove gnome-taquin
```

GNOME CHARACTER MAP APPLICATION

It is a free, open-source Unicode character map program and simple utility application to find and insert unusual characters, part of GNOME. The program allows characters to be displayed by Unicode block or script type. It allows to quickly find the character you are looking for by searching for keywords and includes descriptions of related symbols and meanings of the nature in question. It is formerly known as Gucharmap. It can also input or enter characters. The search functionality allows several search methods, including Unicode name or code point of the essence. It is built on GTK toolkit that can run on any platform supported by GTK. Several text programs use Gucharmap for character input.

You can also browse characters by categories such as Punctuation, Pictures, etc.

Now, run the update command to update repositories and get latest package information.

```
$ sudo apt-get update -y
```

You need to run the install command with -y flag to quickly install the packages and dependencies (see the following figure).

```
$ sudo apt-get install -y gnome-characters
```

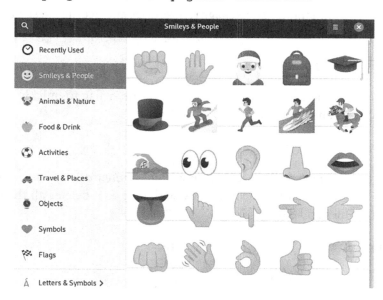

Gnome-characters Application window.

SOUND-JUICER APPLICATION

The application Sound-Juicer is a CD ripping tool using GTK+ and GStreamer.20-Feb-2018. Sound-Juicer is a CD ripper and player for GNOME, which aims to have a simple, clean, easy to use interface. Sound-Juicer supports encoding to several popular audio formats such as Ogg Vorbis and FLAC, additional formats can add through GStreamer plugins. It was written by Ross Burton.

First, update your system with the command:

```
$ sudo apt-get update
```

The above command will download the package lists for Ubuntu 16.04 on your system. It will update the list of the newest versions of packages and their dependencies on your system.

After downloading the latest package list with the help of the above, you can run the installation process.

After the update, use the following command to install Sound-Juicer:

```
$ sudo apt-get install sound-juicer
```

The above command will confirm before installing the package on your Ubuntu GNOME system. If you are not logged in as su, the installer will ask you for the root password. After completing the installation, you can use the package on your system.

To Uninstall or Remove Sound-Juicer

Now, the commands for uninstalling the Sound-Juicer from GNOME. You can use the apt command and remove the package from the system for uninstalling this package.

To remove the Sound-Juicer following command is used:

```
$ sudo apt-get remove
sound-juicer
```

The following command is used to remove the Sound-Juicer package along with its dependencies:

```
$ sudo apt-get remove --auto-remove sound-juicer
```

PHOTOS APPLICATION

You can access, organize, and share your photos on GNOME. A simple and elegant replacement for using a file manager to deal with photo applications. It helps to enhance, crop, and edit in a snap. It seamless cloud integration is offered through GNOME Online Accounts.

- You can do various things by using photos

- You can automatically find all your pictures

- You can view recent local and online photos

- Access your Facebook or Flickr pictures

- You can view photos on TVs, laptops, or other DLNA renderers on your local network

- Set pictures as your desktop background

- Print photos

Select favorites and edit your pictures in the app, or send them to a full-featured editor for more advanced changes.

Installation
First, update your system with the command:

```
$ sudo apt-get update
```

The above command will download the package lists for Ubuntu 16.04 on your system. It will update the list of the newest versions of packages and their dependencies on your system.

Install GNOME-photos Package
Here is a brief guide to show you how to install the GNOME-photos package:

```
$ sudo apt Install gnome-photos
```

Run the Application using command:

```
$ gnome-photos
```

The output will be as shown in the following figure.

Photos
Access, organize and share your photos on GNOME

Install

GNOME-photos Application window.

To Uninstall or Remove GNOME-photos Package

Please follow the step-by-step instructions below to uninstall the GNOME-photos package:

```
$ sudo apt remove gnome-photos
$ sudo apt autoclean && sudo apt autoremove
```

BLANKET APPLICATION

The blanket is a new desktop app for Linux designed solely to play background noises like nature sounds, indistinct ambient noise, white noise, and pink noise. Nothing more, nothing less.

Listening to background noise is a staple life hack. It can help slow a speeding mind. It can help dial out distractions around you. And it can wrap you up with a sense of familiarity and safety.

Blanket allows you to play multiple background sounds at the same time. It means you can create your own custom ambient noise mixes. You can adjust the volume of each sound stream independently, ideal for creating a multi-layer wall of relaxing sounds.

The blanket is free, open-source software with source code available on Github.

Install Blanket

Open terminal from your system app launcher, then run the command to add the PPA given below:

```
$ sudo add-apt-repository ppa:apandada1/blanket
```

Type user password when it asks and hit Enter to continue.
    After that, run the apt command to install it:

```
$ sudo apt install blanket
```

Once it is installed, open it from the system app launcher and enjoy!

To Uninstall Blanket

To remove the PPA, either go to Software & Updates -> Other Software or run the command:

```
$ sudo add-apt-repository --remove ppa:apandada1/
blanket
```

To remove the noise player, run the command:

```
$ sudo apt remove --auto-remove blanket
```

The blanket is a GTK application that allows to play some ambient sounds, including:

- Birdsong

- Summer night

- Rain, storm, wind.

- Coffee shop, fireplace.

- White noise, pink noise.

- Train, boat, and city.

JUNCTION APPLICATION

This Application lets you choose the Application to open files and links.

After installing, make sure to launch the Application.

The Junction will pop up automatically when you open a link in a desktop application. Use the mouse or keyboard navigation to choose the Application to open the link or file.

Features

- Choose the Application to open with

- Show the location before opening

- Edit the URL before opening

- Show a hint for insecure link

- Keyboard navigation

- Middle-click to open in multiple applications

Usage

- You can set Junction as the default application for a resource and let it do the rest. The Junction will pop up and offer multiple options to handle it.

- Set Junction as the default browser, default for all files, the default for png, default email composer, set Junction as default folder opener.

- API.

Tips and Tricks

- Keyboard navigation

- Open with multiple applications

- You can make Junction appear in the center of the screen

- Also can use Junction from the terminal

- Add custom scripts to Junction

- Browser integration

- Multiple Firefox profiles

Install fonts-junction Software

First, update your system with the command:

```
$ sudo apt-get update
```

The above command will download the package lists for Ubuntu 16.04 on your system. It will update the list of the newest versions of packages and their dependencies on your system.

You can install in your Ubuntu GNOME by running the commands given below on the terminal:

```
$ sudo apt-get install fonts-junction
```

TANGRAM APPLICATION

It is a browser that aims to help you run and manage web applications in Linux. It is a new browser designed to organize and run Web applications. Each tab is independent. You can set various tabs with different accounts for a single application. If you want something that only focuses on web application experience, Tangram is an option.

Installing Tangram in Linux

It's available as a Flatpak for all major distributions, and it's also in AUR. Utilize the following command to install it if you want to use the terminal:

First, update your system with the command:

```
$ sudo apt-get update
```

The above command will download the package lists for Ubuntu 16.04 on your system. It will update the list of the newest versions of packages and their dependencies on your system.

Installation

Open Software Application, and then search "Tangram" application. Then click install.

Features

- It's a WebKitGTK-based minimalist browser.

- Here is the list of the features. Here's what you can do:

- You can re-order tabs in the sidebar

- You can add any web service as a web app

- Ability to tweak the user agent on Desktop/mobile)

- Keyboard shortcuts

- Also, change the position of the sidebar (tab bar)

SHORTWAVE APPLICATION

An Internet radio player provides a station database with over 25,000 stations.

Features

- It can create your library where you can add your favorite stations

- It can easily search and discover new radio stations

- It can provide automatic recognition of songs, with the possibility to save them individually

- Responsive application layout, compatible for small and large screens

- Can play audio on supported network devices (e.g., Google Chromecasts)

- Seamless integration into the GNOME desktop environment

First, update your system with the command:

```
$ sudo apt-get update
```

The above command will download the package lists for Ubuntu 16.04 on your system. It will update the list of the newest versions of packages and their dependencies on your system.

You can install in your Ubuntu GNOME by running the commands given below on the terminal:

```
user@user-VirtualBox:~$ snap install shortwave
shortwave 1.1.1 from Alex Murray (alexmurray)
installed
```

When you open this application the output will be as shown in the following figure.

Shortwave Application window.

GBRAINY APPLICATION

It is a game that trainer to have fun and to keep your brain trained gbrainy is a platform to train memory, arithmetical and logical capabilities with many different exercises of different levels. It should do something for all ages and purposes such as kids whose parents want them to develop their abilities, adults that want to keep their mind in form or try it out for fun, older people that might need to do some memory exercises, etc.

Install gbrainy Architecture

First, update your system with the command:

```
$ sudo apt-get update
```

The above command will download the package lists for Ubuntu GNOME on your system. It will update the list of the newest versions of packages and their dependencies on your system.

Install gbrainy Architecture

After the update, use the following command to install gbrainy Architecture:

```
$ sudo apt-get install gbrainy
```

To uninstall or remove gbrainy Architecture:
To remove the gbrainy Architecture following command is used:

```
$ sudo apt-get remove
gbrainy
```

The following command is used to remove the gbrainy Architecture package along with its dependencies:

```
$ sudo apt-get remove --auto-remove gbrainy
```

Completely removing gbrainy Architecture:
The following command should be used with care as it deletes all the configuration files and data:

```
$ sudo apt-get purge gbrainy
```

or you can use following command also:

```
$ sudo apt-get purge --auto-remove gbrainy
```

It is a brain teaser game and trainer to have fun and train your brain.
It provides the following types of games:

- Logic puzzles. These games are designed to challenge your reasoning and thinking skills.

- Mental calculation. These games based on arithmetical operations are designed to prove your mental calculation skills.

- Memory trainers. Games designed to challenge your short-term memory.

- Verbal analogies. These games challenge your verbal aptitude.

- It provides different difficulty levels making gbrainy enjoyable for kids, adults, or senior citizens. It also features players' game history, records, tips for the player, or full screen mode. It can extend easily with new games developed by third-party.

- It is for GNOME and runs on top of GNU-Linux and different Unix flavors.

gbrainy Project Objectives

- A free and open brain teaser game for Linux, Windows, and other platforms.

- Bring a platform that other people can build up their applications or clients.

- A collection of free and brain teasers described using XML that any other application can consume to the author.

GAJIM'S APPLICATION

The goal is to provide a full-featured and easy-to-use Jabber client. It was released under the GNU General Public License. It works well with GNOME but does not require it to run.

Install Instructions

Available in Ubuntu packages and Debian packages.

```
$ sudo apt install gajim
```

The plugin packages are available for the Ubuntu Desktop environment NOME. We recommend installing Gajim plugins on Ubuntu/Debian via packages to resolve dependencies automatically.

To install Gajim's OMEMO plugin, for example:

```
$ sudo apt install gajim-omemo
```

Features

- Tabbed chat window

- Group chat support (with MUC protocol)

- Emoticons, Avatars, File Transfer, Room Bookmarks

- Metal contacts Support

- Trayicon, Speller, extended chat History other functionalities

- TLS and GPG support

- Support transport Registration

- Service Discovery including Nodes

- Wikipedia, dictionary, and search engine lookup

- Support multiple accounts

- DBus Capabilities

- XML Console

- Gajim is available in 27 languages: Basque, Belarusian, Brasilian, Breton, British, Bulgarian, Chinese, Croatian, Czech, Danish, Dutch, English, Esperanto, French, Galician, German, Greek, Italian, Lithuanian, Norwegian, Polish, Portuguese, Russian, Serbian, Spanish, Slovak, and Swedish

KHRONOS-API APPLICATION

The Khronos Vulkan API is a vivid, low-overhead, cross-platform graphics and computes API. Vulkan provides applications with control over the system execution and memory to maximize application efficiency on various devices, from PCs and consoles to mobile phones and embedded platforms.

The Khronos contains specifications, header files, extension specifications, enumerate and function registries, and other related documentation for Khronos APIs, Languages, and associated products.

The Khronos API guide, available in HTML and PDF versions, provides guidelines for implementers of OpenGL ES, OpenVG, and other API standards specified by the Khronos Group. One of the goals is to allow an application binary to run on top of numerous other OpenGL ES/OpenVG/ EGL implementations on the same platform.

The package contains the Khronos XML API Registry and is the successor to the old and undocumented .spec files used for many years to describe the GL, WGL, and GLX APIs.

Install khronos-api Using apt-get

First, update your system with the command. There are three ways to install khronos-api on Ubuntu GNOME 18.04. We can use apt-get, apt, and aptitude. In the following, we will describe each method. You can choose one of them.

After updating the apt database, We can install khronos-api using apt-get by running the following command:

```
$ sudo apt-get -y install khronos-api
```

The above command will download the package lists for Ubuntu GNOME on your system. It will update the list of the newest versions of packages and their dependencies on your system.

Install khronos-api

After the update, use the following command to install khronos-api:

```
$ sudo apt-get install khronos-api
```

To Uninstall or Remove khronos-api

To remove the khronos-api following command is used:

```
$ sudo apt-get remove
khronos-api
```

The following command is used to remove the khronos-api package along with its dependencies:

```
$ sudo apt-get remove --auto-remove khronos-api
```

Completely Removing khronos-api

The following command should be used with care as it deletes all the configuration files and data:

```
$ sudo apt-get purge khronos-api
```

or you can use the following command also:

```
$ sudo apt-get purge --auto-remove khronos-api
```

or

```
$ sudo apt-get remove khronos-api
```

Install khronos-api Using Aptitude

You may need to install aptitude first if you wish to use this approach, as aptitude is not normally installed by default on Ubuntu. Aptitude can use to update the apt database using the following command.

```
$ sudo aptitude update
```

After updating the apt database, We can install khronos-api using aptitude by running the following command:

```
$ sudo aptitude -y install khronos-api
```

To Remove khronos-api Configurations and Data

To remove khronos-api configuration and data from Ubuntu 18.04, we can use the following command:

```
$ sudo apt-get -y purge khronos-api
```

To Remove khronos-api Configuration, Data, and All of Its Dependencies

We can use the following command to remove khronos-api configurations, data and all of its dependencies, we can use the following command:

```
$ sudo apt-get -y autoremove --purge khronos-api
```

ABIWORD APPLICATION

It is a free, well-featured, cross-platform word processor part of the GNOME Project. The default GNOME word processor free office suite GNOME Office remains a standalone application.

While AbiWord is a word processor capable of many different word processing tasks; it is not installed as default in Ubuntu since Ubuntu uses the potent OpenOffice instead. AbiWord is a very lightweight word processor compared to full-featured suites like OpenOffice. It is the default word processor in the Ubuntu derivative Xubuntu.

Since Ubuntu is focused on stability, you will find that, apart from security updates and bug fixes, the AbiWord package in the repositories will generally only be updated to a newer version with every new release Ubuntu.

Install AbiWord Using apt-get

First, update your system with the command. There are three ways to install abiword on Ubuntu GNOME 18.04. We can use apt-get, apt, and aptitude. In the following, we will describe each method. You can choose one of them.

After updating the apt database, We can install abiword using apt-get by running the following command:

```
$ sudo apt-get -y install abiword
```

The above command will download the package lists for Ubuntu GNOME on your system. It will update the list of the newest versions of packages and their dependencies on your system.

Install AbiWord

After the update, use the following command to install abiword:

```
$ sudo apt-get install abiword
```

Run the application using abiword, as shown in the following figure.

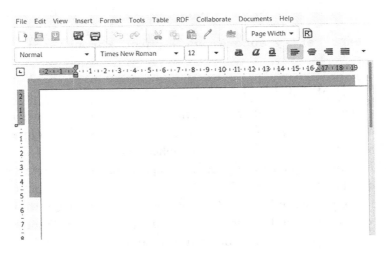

AbiWord Application window.

To Uninstall or Remove AbiWord

To remove the abiword following command is used:

```
$ sudo apt-get remove
abiword
```

The following command is used to remove theabiword package along with its dependencies:

```
$ sudo apt-get remove --auto-remove abiword
```

Completely Removing AbiWord

The following command should be used with care as it deletes all the configuration files and data:

```
$ sudo apt-get purge abiword
```

or you can use the following command also:

```
$ sudo apt-get purge --auto-remove abiword
```

or

```
$ sudo apt-get remove abiword
$ sudo apt autoclean && sudo apt autoremove
```

Install abiword Using Aptitude

You may need to install aptitude first if you wish to use this approach, as aptitude is not normally installed by default on Ubuntu. Aptitude can be used to update the apt database using the following command.

```
$ sudo aptitude update
```

After updating the apt database, We can install abiword using aptitude by running the following command:

```
$sudo aptitude -y install abiword
```

To Remove AbiWord Configurations and Data

To remove abiword configuration and data from Ubuntu GNOME, we can use the following command:

```
$ sudo apt-get -y purge abiword
```

To Remove AbiWord Configuration, Data, and All of Its Dependencies

We can use the following command to remove abiword configurations, data, and all of its dependencies, we can use the following command:

```
$ sudo apt-get -y autoremove --purge abiword
```

Install AbiWord from the Repository

The easy way to install AbiWord is using the official Ubuntu repositories. That way, you will get a stable version, which is supported by Canonical Ltd. as well as the Ubuntu community.

Installing using the repositories is pretty straightforward:

- Go to Applications, Add/Remove.

- Search for AbiWord and tick the box with AbiWord.

- Press Apply Changes and, if asked, enter your password.

GNUMERIC APPLICATION

Gnumeric can start in several ways, depending on your computer operating system and desktop environment.

Gnumeric from the GNOME Desktop

You should have a "panel" on your desktop if you are working on the GNOME system. The panel contains icons and at least two menus. These menus are called Applications and have an icon that looks like a foot's outline. If you click on the menu name, then the menu will appear. Drag the cursor down to the sub-menu name, and a sub-menu will appear. You can also Drag the cursor into the sub-menu and then release the mouse button when the cursor is on the entry, which reads "Gnumeric Spreadsheet."

Install Gnumeric Using apt-get

First, update your system with the command. There are three ways to install Gnumeric on Ubuntu GNOME. We can use apt-get, apt, and aptitude. In the following, we will describe each method. You can choose one of them.

After updating the apt database, We can install Gnumeric using apt-get by running the following command:

```
$ sudo apt-get -y install gnumeric
```

The above command will download the package lists for Ubuntu GNOME on your system. It will update the list of the newest versions of packages and their dependencies on your system.

Install Gnumeric

After the update, use the following command to install Gnumeric:

```
$ sudo apt-get install gnumeric
```

To Uninstall or Remove Gnumeric

To remove the Gnumeric following command is used:

```
$ sudo apt-get remove
gnumeric
```

The following command is used to remove the Gnumeric package along with its dependencies:

```
$ sudo apt-get remove --auto-remove gnumeric
```

Completely Removing Gnumeric

The following command should be used with care as it deletes all the configuration files and data:

```
$ sudo apt-get purge gnumeric
```

or you can use the following command also:

```
$ sudo apt-get purge --auto-remove gnumeric
```

or

```
$ sudo apt-get remove gnumeric
$ sudo apt autoclean && sudo apt autoremove
```

Install Gnumeric Using Aptitude

If you want to use this approach, you'll probably need to install aptitude first, as it's not often installed by default on Ubuntu. Using aptitude, update the apt database.

```
$ sudo aptitude update
```

After updating the apt database, We can install Gnumeric using aptitude by running the following command:

```
$ sudo aptitude -y install gnumeric
```

To Remove Gnumeric Configurations and Data

We may use the following command to remove Gnumeric settings and data from Ubuntu GNOME:

```
$ sudo apt-get -y purge gnumeric
```

To Remove Gnumeric Configuration, Data, and All of Its Dependencies

We can use the following command to remove Gnumeric configurations, data, and all of its dependencies, and we can use the following command:

```
$ sudo apt-get -y autoremove --purge gnumeric
```

Gnumeric can open using a spreadsheet file directly. If there is any spreadsheet file on the desktop, it can double-click with the mouse pointer on the file and have Gnumeric open the file automatically. Alternatively, you can able to right-click on the file and get a pop-up menu that will allow you to select Gnumeric as the application to open the file (see the following figure).

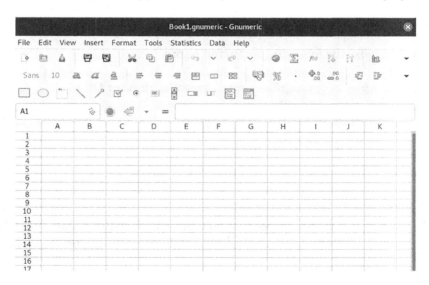

Gnumeric Application window.

The application contains a menubar at the top, two toolbars below the menu bar. On the left, there is an object toolbar. The data entry area the cell grid area is on the right, which is above the list of worksheets and the information area.

1. The menubar
   It provides access to the core functions of GNOME. You can do almost everything you can do in Gnumeric through the menus.

2. The format toolbar
   It changes the display properties of data in the workbook.

3. The object toolbar
   This toolbar allows you to draw graphic elements on the sheet, such as text labels, big red circles, or thin green arrows, and you can use these to bring attention to a particular worksheet part.

4. The data entry area
   The data entry area is helpful for the modification of complex formulas.

   • The cell grid area
     The area lies in the middle of all the rest includes the row and column labels, the scrollbars, and the tabs.

   • The information area
     Gnumeric uses this area to give you feedback on the status of specific operations.

AUDACIOUS AUDIO PLAYER APPLICATION

It is a free, advanced audio player for Linux and many other Unix-compatible systems that focus on low resource usage, high audio quality, and support for a wide range of audio formats. It was initially based on Beep Media Player, based on XMMS.

This section will describe two ways to install Audacious on Ubuntu. You can choose based on the source you want to install Audacious from and if you want to use the UI or the command line.

   • Using Ubuntu Software Manager

   • Using Command-Line the Terminal

Install Audacious from PPA via the Command Line

The PPA repository includes the latest version of Audacious. Follow these steps to install Audacious through this PPA repository.

Install Audacious

First, please open the Terminal through the system the Ctrl + Alt + T shortcut.

Enter the following command to add the Nilarimogard PPA repository to your Ubuntu:

```
$ sudo add-apt-repository ppa:nilarimogard/webupd8
```

Only an authorized system user can add, remove, and configure software on the Ubuntu GNOME system. Then they will ask for the password, enter the password for sudo, after which the PPA repository will add to your system.

Instead of typing the command, you can simply copy it from here and paste it into the Terminal by using the Ctrl + Shift + V or the Paste option from the right-click menu.

The further step is to update the system repository through the following command:

```
$ sudo apt-get update
```

Now, you are done with adding the PPA, use the following command as sudo to install Audacious and its plugins to your system:

```
$ sudo apt-get install audacious audacious-plugins
```

The system might prompt with a y/n option to continue the installation. Type Y and press enter if you want to continue with the installation. Depending on the Internet speed, the process might take some time, after which Audacious will be installed on your system.

The following command will let you check your installed package's version number and ensure that the software is indeed installed on your system.

```
$ audacious --version
```

Launch Audacious

You can launch Audacious through the Ubuntu UI or by entering the following command in the Terminal:

```
$ audacious
```

The output will be as shown in the following figure.

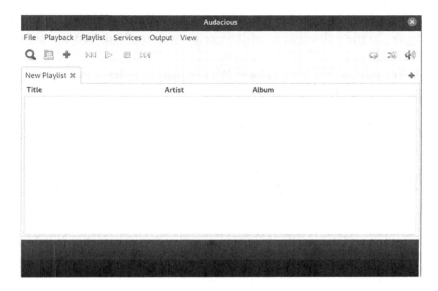

Audacious Application window.

To Remove Software

You can use the following command in your Terminal to uninstall Audacious and its plugins from your system:

```
$ sudo apt-get remove audacious audacious-plugins
```

Enter y when you see the y/n prompt, and the software will remove it from your system altogether.

If you also want to remove the PPA through which you installed Audacious, run the following command as sudo:

```
$ sudo add-apt-repository --remove ppa:nilarimogard/
webupd8
```

Alexandria is a collection of utilities in the public domain for Common Lisp. It is a library but also a project that aims to reduce duplication of effort and improve the portability of Common Lisp code according to its own characteristic and rather conservative aesthetic. It is used by other projects as a base to build on.

Install cl-alexandria Using apt-get

First, update your system with the command. There are three ways to install cl-alexandria on Ubuntu GNOME. We can use apt-get, apt, and aptitude. In the following, we will describe each method. You can choose one of them.

After updating the apt database, We can install cl-alexandria using apt-get by running the following command:

```
$ sudo apt-get -y install cl-alexandria
```

The above command will download the package lists for Ubuntu GNOME on your system. It will update the list of the newest versions of packages and their dependencies on your system.

Install cl-alexandria

After the update, use the following command to install cl-alexandria:

```
$ sudo apt-get install cl-alexandria
```

To uninstall or remove cl-alexandria

To remove the cl-alexandria following command is used:

```
$ sudo apt-get remove
cl-alexandria
```

The following command is used to remove the cl-alexandria package along with its dependencies:

```
$ sudo apt-get remove --auto-remove cl-alexandria
```

Completely Removing cl-alexandria

The following command should be used with care as it deletes all the configuration files and data:

```
$ sudo apt-get purge cl-alexandria
```

or you can use the following command also:

```
$ sudo apt-get purge --auto-remove cl-alexandria
```

or

```
$ sudo apt-get remove cl-alexandria
$ sudo apt autoclean && sudo apt autoremove
```

Install cl-alexandria Using Aptitude

Because aptitude is not normally installed by default on Ubuntu, you may need to install it first. The following command will update the apt database with aptitude.

```
$ sudo aptitude update
```

After updating the apt database, We can install cl-alexandria using aptitude by running the following command:

```
$ sudo aptitude -y install cl-alexandria
```

To Remove cl-alexandria Configurations and Data

To remove cl-alexandria configuration and data from Ubuntu GNOME, we can use the following command:

```
$ sudo apt-get -y purge cl-alexandria
```

To Remove cl-alexandria Configuration, Data, and All of Its Dependencies

We can use the following command to remove cl-alexandria configurations, data, and all of its dependencies, and we can use the following command:

```
$ sudo apt-get -y autoremove --purge cl-alexandria
```

Features

- Retrieves and displays book information from several online libraries such as Amazon, Proxis, British Library, and Barnes and Noble.

- It allows books to be added and updated manually.

- Shows books in different views (standard list or icons list), filtered, and sorted.

GNOME DICTIONARY APPLICATION

It is a dictionary application that looks up definitions of words online, and it looks up English definitions by default. You can easily switch to Spanish or add other dictionaries using the DICT protocol to suit your needs.

Install GNOME-dictionary using apt-get

First, update your system with the command. There are three ways to install GNOME-dictionary on Ubuntu GNOME. We can use apt-get, apt, and aptitude. In the following, we will describe each method. You can choose one of them.

After updating the apt database, we can install GNOME-dictionary using apt-get by running the following command:

```
$ sudo apt-get -y install gnome-dictionary
```

or you can also you the snapd to install the gome-dictionary (see the following figure).

```
$ sudo snap install gnome-dictionary
```

GNOME Dictionary Application window.

The above command will download the package lists for Ubuntu GNOME on your system. It will update the list of the newest versions of packages and their dependencies on your system.

Install GNOME-dictionary

After the update, use the following command to install GNOME-dictionary:

```
$ sudo apt-get install gnome-dictionary
```

To Uninstall or Remove GNOME-dictionary

To remove the GNOME-dictionary following command is used:

```
$ sudo apt-get remove
GNOME-dictionary
```

or you can also use the snapd command to remove.

```
$ sudo snap remove gnome-dictionary
```

The following command is used to remove the GNOME-dictionary package along with its dependencies:

```
$ sudo apt-get remove --auto-remove gnome-dictionary
```

Completely removing GNOME-dictionary:

The following command should be used with care as it deletes all the configuration files and data:

```
$ sudo apt-get purge gnome-dictionary
```

or you can use the following command also:

```
$ sudo apt-get purge --auto-remove gnome-dictionary
```

or

```
$ sudo apt-get remove gnome-dictionary
$ sudo apt autoclean && sudo apt autoremove
```

Install GNOME-dictionary Using Aptitude

You may need to install aptitude first if you want to use this approach, as aptitude is not normally installed by default on Ubuntu. Aptitude can be used to update the apt database using the following command.

```
$ sudo aptitude update
```

After updating the apt database, we can install GNOME-dictionary using aptitude by running the following command:

```
$ sudo aptitude -y install gnome-dictionary
```

To Remove GNOME-dictionary Configurations and Data

To remove GNOME-dictionary configuration and data from Ubuntu GNOME, we can use the following command:

```
$ sudo apt-get -y purge gnome-dictionary
```

To Remove GNOME-dictionary Configuration, Data, and All of Its Dependencies

We can use the following command to remove GNOME-dictionary configurations, data, and all of its dependencies, and we can use the following command:

```
$ sudo apt-get -y autoremove --purge gnome-dictionary
```

A Color-Picker and Editor for Web Designers and Digital Artists

Color-Picker is an advanced screen color picker based on Qt's QColorDialog library, A color picker and color editor for web designers and digital artists, created by designers and digital artists. With Color Picker, identifying the colors, saving, etc., is a quick and easy job.

Color-Picker features include:

- Five formats of color codes: HTML, HexRGBA, RGB, HSB/HSV, CMYK, and their variations. Conversion of HTML, HEX, and RGB color codes into the corresponding colors.

- Color-Picker for easy handling and greater precision.

- A Color list is used for saving and reusing the picked color samples for each picked color.

- Color preview widget.

- Progressive color pattern generator.

- Support Switching three themes – System, Flat Light, and Dark.

Enable Snaps on Install Color-Picker

Snaps are applications packaged with dependencies to run on all popular distributions from a single build. They need to be updated automatically and roll back gracefully.

Snaps are installable from the Snap Store, an app store with an audience of millions.

A snap can install from the Ubuntu Software Centre by searching for snaps. snapd can install from the command line as given below:

```
$ sudo apt update
$ sudo apt install snapd
```

You can log-out and back in again or restart your system to ensure snap's paths are updated correctly.

Install Color-Picker

To install Color-Picker, use the following command:

```
$ sudo snap install color-picker
```

To Remove or Uninstall Color-Picker

```
$ sudo snap remove color-picker
```

EMPATHY APPLICATION

Install Empathy Using apt-get

First, update your system with the command. There are three ways to install empathy on Ubuntu GNOME. We can use apt-get, apt, and aptitude. In the following, we will describe each method. You can choose one of them.

After updating the apt database, We can install empathy using apt-get by running the following command:

```
$ sudo apt-get -y install empathy
```

or you can also use the snapd to install the empathy

```
$ sudo snap install empathy
```

The above command will download the package lists for Ubuntu GNOME on your system. It will update the list of the newest versions of packages and their dependencies on your system.

Install Empathy

After the update, use the following command to install empathy:

```
$ sudo apt-get install empathy
```

To Uninstall or Remove Empathy

To remove the empathy following command is used:

```
$ sudo apt-get remove
empathy
```

or you can also use the snapd command to remove

```
$ sudo snap remove empathy
```

The following command is used to remove the empathy package along with its dependencies:

```
$ sudo apt-get remove --auto-remove empathy
```

Completely Removing Empathy

The following command should be used with care as it deletes all the configuration files and data:

```
$ sudo apt-get purge empathy
```

or you can use the following command also:

```
$ sudo apt-get purge --auto-remove empathy
```

or

```
$ sudo apt-get remove empathy
$ sudo apt autoclean && sudo apt autoremove
```

Install Empathy Using Aptitude

You may need to install aptitude first if you want to use this approach, as aptitude is not normally installed by default on Ubuntu. Aptitude can be used to update the apt database using the following command:

```
$ sudo aptitude update
```

After updating the apt database, We can install empathy using aptitude by running the following command:

```
$ sudo aptitude -y install empathy
```

The window of the application looks like as shown in the following figure.

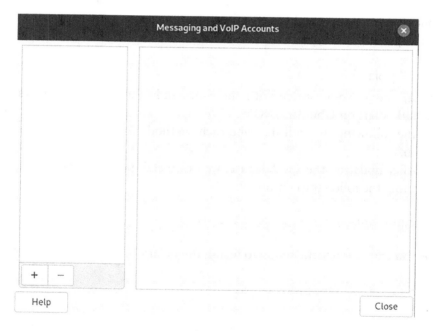

Empathy Application window.

To Remove Empathy Configurations and Data

To remove empathyconfiguration and data from Ubuntu GNOME, we can use the following command:

```
$ sudo apt-get -y purge empathy
```

Delete Empathy Configuration, Data, and All of
Its Dependencies

We can use the following command to remove empathy configurations, data, and all of its dependencies, and we can use the following
command:

```
$ sudo apt-get -y autoremove --purge empathy
```

POLARI APPLICATION

A simple Internet Relay Chat (IRC) client designed to integrate seamlessly
with GNOME features a beautiful and straightforward interface that
allows you to focus on your conversations.

You can use Polari to chat with people publicly and have private one-to-
one conversations in a channel and notifications make sure that never miss
an important message.

Install polari Using apt-get

First, update your system with the command. There are three ways to
install polari on Ubuntu GNOME. We can use apt-get, apt, and aptitude.
In the following, we will describe each method. You can choose one of
them.

After updating the apt database, we can install polari using apt-get by
running the following command:

```
$ sudo apt-get -y install polari
```

or you can also use the snapd to install the polari

```
$ sudo snap install polari
```

The above command will download the package lists for Ubuntu GNOME
on your system. It will update the list of the newest versions of packages
and their dependencies on your system.

Install polari

After the update, use the following command to install polari:

```
$ sudo apt-get install polari
```

To run the polar double click on the icon and the output will be as shown in the following figure.

Polari Application window.

To Uninstall or Remove polari

To remove the polari, the following command is used:

```
$ sudo apt-get remove
polari
```

or you can also use the snapd command to remove

```
$ sudo snap remove polari
```

The following command is used to remove the polari package along with its dependencies:

```
$ sudo apt-get remove --auto-remove polari
```

Completely Removing polari

The following command should be used with care as it deletes all the configuration files and data:

```
$ sudo apt-get purge polari
```

or you can use the following command also:

```
$ sudo apt-get purge --auto-remove polari
```

or

```
$ sudo apt-get remove polari
$ sudo apt autoclean && sudo apt autoremove
```

Install polari Using Aptitude

You may need to install aptitude first if you want to use this approach, as aptitude is not normally installed by default on Ubuntu. Aptitude can be used to update the apt database using the following command.

```
$ sudo aptitude update
```

After updating the apt database, We can install polari using aptitude by running the following command:

```
$ sudo aptitude -y install polari
```

To Remove polari Configurations and Data

To remove polari and data from Ubuntu GNOME, we can use the following command:

```
$ sudo apt-get -y purge polari
```

Polari's configuration, data, and all of its dependencies should remove.

To delete polari settings, data, and all of their dependencies, we may use the following command:

```
$ sudo apt-get -y autoremove --purge polari
```

VINO VNC APPLICATION

Enable Screen Sharing on Ubuntu

VNC is a protocol used to access a computer's graphical desktop environment and control it from a remote computer.

Installing VNC Server on Ubuntu

In the GNOME desktop environment built-in Screen Sharing feature allows remote access to the Ubuntu 20.04 LTS graphical desktop environment.

The GNOME desktop uses the Vino VNC server to execute the Screen Sharing function.

By default, the Vino VNC server might not be installed on your Ubuntu 20.04 LTS operating system. But it is also available in the official repository of Ubuntu GNOME. So, you can install it easily.

First, update the APT package repository cache with the following command:

```
$ sudo apt update
```

To install Vino, run the following command as given below:

```
$ sudo apt install vino
```

When you run the application the output will be as shown in the following figure.

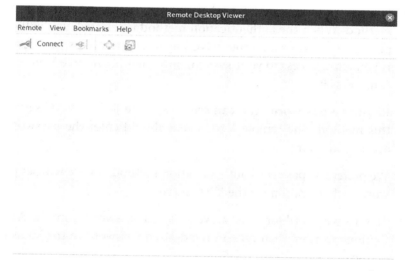

Vino Application window.

To further installation, press Y and then press <Enter>. Vimo will be installed.

Enable Screen Sharing on Ubuntu

- Once Vino is installed, you should enable the Screen Sharing option from the Settings app.

- Then, open the Settings from the Application Menu of Ubuntu GNOME.

- Navigate to the Sharing section and click on the toggle button as the screenshot below to enable Sharing.

  - Filename = Screen Sharing.PNG

  - Caption = Screen Sharing

- Once Sharing is turned on, click on Screen Sharing.

- Click on the toggle button to enable Screen Sharing from the Screen Sharing window.

- Screen Sharing should enable in your system.

- You can configure authentication methods as per your VNC server from the Access Options section.

- For new connections, must ask for access: As default authentication method. When the authentication method is selected, you will get a prompt every time a remote VNC client tries to access your system. If you allow access to your system, only then the remote VNC client can access it.

- **Require a password:** You can set a password for the VNC server in this method. The remote VNC client should enter the password to access your computer.

- We prefer the password authentication method. So, we will set password authentication for the VNC server.

- To set a password for VNC server, select a password from the Access Options section, then type in the desired password in the Password textbox.

- Accessing Your Computer Remotely with Vinagre:

  - The Vinagre remote desktop client shows you how to connect to your computer via VNC. Also, you can use other VNC clients.

  - The Vinagre remote desktop may not install on the system. If you need help for installation Vinagre on your Linux distribution, you can install it using the above command.

- First, open Vinagre remote desktop from the Application Menu of your system.

- Once Vinagre is opened, click on Connect.

- Now, select VNC from the Protocol dropdown menu, type in the IP address of your remote computer in the Host textbox, and click on Connect as marked in the screenshot below.

- You will be asked for the VNC password if you have configured password authentication.

- Type in your VNC authentication password and click on Authenticate as marked. You should be connected to your Ubuntu 20.04 LTS computer remotely.

Evolution Logo, Evolution Mail, and Calendar

By default, Evolution opens the mail view, where you can view all your mail. You can change to other application views by going to the bottom of the left pane in the window (the so-called "switcher") and selecting the desired view.

Install Evolution Using apt-get

First, update your system with the command. There are three ways to install Evolution on Ubuntu GNOME. We can use apt-get, apt, and aptitude. In the following, we will describe each method. You can choose one of them.

After updating the apt database, we can install Evolution using apt-get by running the following command:

```
$ sudo apt-get -y install Evolution
```

or you can also use the snapd to install the Evolution.

```
$ sudo snap install evolution
```

The above command will download the package lists for Ubuntu GNOME on your system. It will update the list of the newest versions of packages and their dependencies on your system.

Install Evolution

After the update, use the following command to install Evolution:

```
$ sudo apt-get install Evolution
```

To Uninstall or Remove Evolution

To remove the Evolution following command is used:

```
$ sudo apt-get remove Evolution
```

or you can also use the snapd command to remove Evolution

```
$ sudo snap remove Evolution
```

The following command is used to remove the Evolution package along with its dependencies:

```
$ sudo apt-get remove --auto-remove evolution
```

Completely Removing Evolution

The following command should be used with care as it deletes all the configuration files and data:

```
$ sudo apt-get purge evolution
```

or you can use the following command also:

```
$ sudo apt-get purge --auto-remove evolution
```

or

```
$ sudo apt-get remove Evolution
$ sudo apt autoclean && sudo apt autoremove
```

Install Evolution Using Aptitude

If you want to follow this method, you might need to install aptitude first since aptitude is usually not installed by default on Ubuntu. Update apt database with aptitude using the following command.

```
$ sudo aptitude update
```

After updating the apt database, We can install Evolution using aptitude by running the following command:

```
$ sudo aptitude -y install Evolution
```

To Remove Evolution Configurations and Data

To remove evolution configuration and data from Ubuntu GNOME, we can use the following command:

```
$ sudo apt-get -y purge evolution
```

To Remove Evolution Configuration, Data, and All of Its Dependencies

We can use the following command to remove Evolution configurations, data, and all of its dependencies, and we can use the following command:

```
$ sudo apt-get -y autoremove --purge evolution
```

CHAPTER SUMMARY

We have discussed the GNOME application, including its working and installation using the command line in your Ubuntu system with user interface guides for each. We also have covered its features and the use of every desktop environment.

CHAPTER 4

Doing More with GNOME

IN THIS CHAPTER

- ➤ Introduction of GTK

- ➤ History of GTK

- ➤ GDK (GIMP Drawing Kit)

- ➤ List of language bindings for GTK

- ➤ Desktop environments based on GTK

- ➤ GTK+

- ➤ Create GUI in GTK Toolkit

The last chapter is all about the application, which is totally based on GNOME. We can install or remove all these applications using the command line and Software application.

Now we will discuss about GTK Toolkit programming in GNOME, basically GTK Toolkit is a library used to create graphical user interfaces (GUIs). It works on UNIX-based platforms, Windows and macOS, where GTK is released under the GNU Library General Public License terms, that allow other for licensing of client applications. GTK has a C-based, object-oriented architecture that allows for maximum flexibility and portability; there are bindings for many other languages, including C++, Objective-C, Guile/Scheme, Perl, Python, JavaScript, Rust, Go, TOM, Ada95, Free Pascal, and Eiffel.

DOI: 10.1201/9781003311942-4

145

INTRODUCTION OF GTK

GTK, i.e., GNU image manipulation program (GIMP) ToolKit, then GTK+, a free and open-source cross-platform widget toolkit for creating GUIs. It is licensed under the GNU General Public License terms, allowing both free and proprietary software to use it. It is one of the most popular toolkits for the Wayland and X11 windowing systems.

It is a multi-platform toolkit for creating GUIs, and you offer a complete set of widgets suitable for projects ranging from small one-off projects to complete application suites.

GTK is a free and open-source software project. The terms for GTK, the GNU LGPL, allow it to be used by all developers, including those developing proprietary software, without any license fees or royalties.

It is necessary to discuss a few topics related to the GTK such as the widget toolkit. So a widget toolkit and library, GUI toolkit, or UX collection of libraries containing a set of graphical control elements called widgets are used to construct programs' graphical user interface (GUI). Most widget toolkits additionally include their rendering engine. This engine can be specific to a particular operating system or windowing system or contains back-ends to interface with multiple ones and renders APIs such as OpenGL, OpenVG, or EGL.

The GTK team releases the latest versions on a regular basis GTK 4 and GTK 3 are maintained, while GTK 2 is at the end.

The GIMP ToolKit (GTK) is a widget toolkit used to create GUIs on various systems GTK is commonly and incorrectly thought to stand for "GNOME ToolKit," but it stands for "GIMP ToolKit" because it was created to design a user interface for GIMP. GTK ToolKit is an object-oriented toolkit written in C (but GTK is not a language). It is entirely open-source under the LGPL license. GTK is a widely-used toolkit for GUIs, and many tools are available for GTK.

Many of you might see the difference between "GTK" and "GTK+." GTK was released first but was not support object-oriented. Later, the GTK developers rewrote the code to make GTK support the object-oriented. After that, they called it "GTK+." However, people still use "GTK" and "GTK+" interchangeably, as you can see in this section. GTK2 and GTK3 refer to GTK versions 2 and 3, respectively. "GTK2", "GTK+ 2", and "GTK2+" all the same is true for GTK3 written in those different styles.

HISTORY OF GTK

Linux

GTK was initially designed and used in the GIMP as a replacement of the Motif toolkit; at some point, Peter Mattis became disenchanted with Motif and began to write his own GUI toolkit named the GIMP toolkit and had successfully replaced Motif by the 0.60 release of GIMP. Finally, it was rewritten to be object-oriented and was renamed GTK+. It was used in the 0.99 release of GIMP. It was maintained by the GNOME Foundation, which uses the GNOME desktop environment.

The GTK 2.0 release series introduced new features, including improved text rendering via Pango, a new theme engine, accessibility using the Accessibility Toolkit, transition to Unicode using UTF-8 strings, and a flexible API. GTK 2 depends on the Cairo 2D graphics library for rendering vector graphics.

GTK version 3.0.0 included as:

- Revised input device handling.

- Support for themes written with CSS-like syntax.

- The ability to get information about other opened GTK applications.

During a Hackathon, the "+" was dropped to simply "GTK" in February 2019.

GUI Designer

A GUI designer is a GUI builder, a software development tool that simplifies the creation of GUIs by allowing the designer to arrange graphical control elements using a drag-and-drop WYSIWYG editor. A GUI must be built by specifying each widget's parameters in the source code.

User interfaces are typically programmed using an event-driven architecture, so GUI builders also simplify creating event-driven code. This supporting code connects widgets with the outgoing and incoming events that trigger the application logic functions.

Some GUI builders can automatically generate the source code for a graphical control element. Others, like Interface Builder or Glade Interface Designer, generate serialized object instances loaded by the application.

Software Architecture of GTK

The library contains a set of graphical control widgets that is elements. Version 3.22.16 includes 186 active and 36 deprecated devices. GTK is an object-oriented widget toolkit written in the programming language C that uses GObject, the GLib object system, for object orientation. While GTK is mainly for window systems based on X11 and Wayland, it works on other platforms, including Microsoft Windows interfaced with the Windows AI and macOS with Quartz. There is also an HTML5 back-end named Broadway.

A library is a collection of implementations of behavior, written in a language, has a well-defined interface by which the behavior is invoked. People who want to write a higher-level program can use a library to make system calls.

The GLib Object System is a free software library providing a portable object system and transparent cross-language interoperability. GObject is designed to use both directly in C programs to provide object-oriented C-based APIs and bindings to other languages to offer transparent cross-language interoperability, e.g., PyGObject (see the following figure).

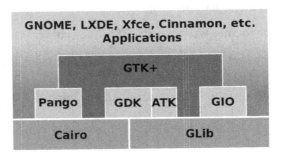

GObject architecture.

The GTK toolkit contains "widgets" like GUI components such as buttons, text input, or windows.

It depends on the following libraries:

- **GLib:** It is a general-purpose utility library, not specific to GUIs. It provides valuable data types, macros, type conversions, string utilities, file utilities, a primary loop abstraction, etc. More information is available on the GLib website.

- **GObject:** It is a library that provides a type system, a collection of fundamental types, including an object type, and a signal system. More information is available on the GObject website.

- **GIO:** A modern, easy-to-use API including abstractions for files, drives, volumes, stream IO, as well as network programming and IPC through DBus. More information is available on the GIO website.

- **Cairo:** It is a 2D-graphics library with support for multiple output devices.

- **OpenGL:** It is an environment for developing portable, interactive 2D and 3D graphics applications.

- **Pango:** It is a library for internationalized text handling. It works around the PangoLayout object, representing a paragraph of text. It provides the engine for GtkTextView, GtkLabel, GtkEntry, and all GTK widgets that display text. More information is available on the Pango website.

- **gdk-pixbuf:** A small, portable library that allows you to create GdkPixbuf objects from image data or image files. We can use GdkPixbuf in combination with widgets like GtkImage to display images.

- **graphene:** A small library that provides vector and matrix data types and operations. It offers optimized implementations using SIMD instruction sets like SSE and ARM NEON.

It is divided into five parts:

1. **GDK:** It is the abstraction layer that allows GTK to support multiple windowing systems and provides window system facilities on Wayland, X11, Microsoft Windows, and Apple macOS.

2. **GSK:** It is an API for creating a scene graph from drawing operation, called "nodes," rendering it using different backends and providing renderers for OpenGL, Vulkan, and Cairo.

3. **GTK:** It is a toolkit containing UI elements, layout managers, data storage types for efficient use in GUI applications, and much more.

4. **ATK:** It is the Accessibility Toolkit that provides a set of generic interfaces allowing accessibility to interact with a GUI. Example, a screen reader uses ATK to discover the text in an interface and read it to blind users. GTK+ widgets have built-in support for accessibility using the ATK framework.

5. **GTK+:** The GTK+ library contains widgets, i.e., GUI components such as GtkButton or GtkTextView.

GIMP DRAWING KIT (GDK)

GDK (short for GIMP Drawing Kit) is a library that acts as a wrapper near the low-level functions provided by the underlying windowing and graphics systems that lies between the display server and the GTK library, handling basic renderings such as drawing primitives, raster graphics (bit-maps), cursors, fonts, window events, and drag-and-drop functionality.

Like GTK Scene Graph Kit (GSK), GDK is part of GTK and licensed under the GNU Lesser General Public License (LGPL).

GDK is an essential encapsulation of standard Xlib function calls (wrapper), and if you're familiar with Xlib, you don't need to be familiar with most GDK functions. All functions provide a convenient style to access the Xlib library function. In addition, GDK used a glib on multiple platforms, and the GDK became more convenient and secure.

Software Architecture

GDK contains back-ends to X11, Wayland, Broadway, Quartz. GDI relies on Cairo for the rendering. Is new scene graph (i.e., canvas) is work-in-progress. Its arrival should herald GTK version 4.0.

GTK implemented on top of an abstraction layer called GDK, freeing GTK from low-level concerns like input gathering, drag and drop, and pixel format conversion. GDK is an intermediate layer that separates GTK from the details of the windowing system (see the following figure).

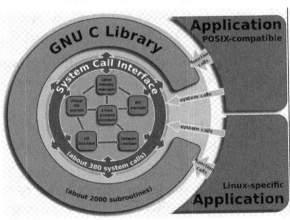

GDK architecture.

GDK is an essential part of GTK's portability. Since GLib already provides low-level cross-platform functionality, all needed to make GTK run on other platforms is to port GDK to the underlying operating system's graphics layer. Hence, it is ported to the Windows API, and Quartz enables GTK applications to run on Windows and macOS, respectively. Starting with GTK+ version 2.8, GDK supports Cairo, which should be used with GTK+ 3 instead of GDK's drawing functions.

GDK is an intermediate layer that isolates GTK from the details of the windowing system and a thin wrapper around Xlib. The X-Window System comes with a low-level library called Xlib. Almost every function in GDK is a fragile wrapper around a corresponding Xlib function. Still, some of the complexity (and functionality) of Xlib is hidden to simplify programming and to make GDK easier to port to other windowing systems such as Wayland or Microsoft Windows. The concealed Xlib functionality will rarely interest application programmers; for example, many features used solely by window managers are not exposed in GDK. GDK lets you do low-level stuff, like, e.g., "blit this pixmap to the screen." GDK provides a much more portable layer than, say, the X protocol without sacrificing any low-level accessibility that systems such as X provide.

Having OpenGL (or OpenGL ES) support in GDK facilitates slightly better control of the graphics pipeline; OpenGL is well suited for compositing textured data but unsuited for drawing.

GdkFrameClock

GdkFrameClock was added in GTK 3.8, while GTK applications remain the main loop driven, the application is idle inside this main loop most of the time and waits for something to happen, and then calls the appropriate subroutine when it does. GdkFrameClock adds a mechanism that gives a "pulse" to the application and tells the application when to update and repaint a window. The beat rate can synchronize with the monitor refresh rate.

GTK Scene Graph Kit

GSK (short for GTK Scene Graph Kit) is the rendering and scene graph API for GTK introduced with version 3.90. GSK lies between the graphical control elements (widgets) and the rendering. Like GDK, GSK is part of GTK and licensed under the GNU LGPL.

GSK is part of GTK. GSK is used by GTK itself and GTK-based applications that wish to replace Clutter for their UI. Applications that used

Clutter instead of using only GTK are, e.g., GNOME Shell, GNOME Videos, GNOME Boxes, and Cheese.

Some points:

- **GUI:** Any application that uses GTK's graphical control elements (widgets), as opposed to those applications getting a GTK window and then drawing themselves on it, benefit from GSK.

- **Performance:** Drawing graphical control elements (widgets) without a scenegraph leads to rendering things that don't show up on the screen, which does not need to be rendered; hence it leads to avoidable performance and battery life losses. The scene graph is used to do hidden surface determination.

- **Simplicity:** The widgets were drawn in GTK (when not using Clutter), which was that a draw function (part of GDK hence the name (GIMP "Drawing" Kit)) drew everything. The current position had to be computed to understand where the mouse pointer was hovering over. With GSK, it should be pretty easy to write complex graphical control elements (widgets) and still track easily the whereabout of the mouse pointer.

GSK Rendering Pipeline
GSK Uses a Dual-Layer Approach
The lower layer is a straightforward rendering tree of operations; it can transform into appropriate rendering commands with minimal state changes, transforming it into the rendering pipeline. GskRenderNode instances represent the tree of rendering operations; an instance of GskRenderer takes the render nodes and submits them to the underlying graphic system.

The higher layer is a complex set of logical layers; it adds a high-level convenience API for application developers.

Rendering APIs
GTK 3.90 is the development version number of what will become GTK 4. GSK supports rendering using these back-ends:

- Cairo

- OpenGL

- Vulkan

GtkInspector

GtkInspector is the preinstalled interactive debugging support in GTK+. It was added in GTK+ 3.14, based on a copy of the well-established gtkparasite. The debugger is disabled by default. To enable it, make sure you have the libgtk-3-dev(debian-naming) or gtk3-devel(fedora-naming) package installed and run in a terminal.

```
$ gsettings set org.gtk.Settings.Debug enable-
inspector-keybinding true
```

Gtkparasite

The Parasite was a delightful project that provided valuable live-debugging tools for GTK-based applications. It was such a success that now it's part of GTK itself.

GtkInspector is the successor to Parasite. It's actively maintained and far more helpful. The Parasite itself has been shut down.

Consider the application you are operating happens to be a Flatpak. At that point, it will probably have a separate GSettings storage than your host system, and you will need to change that environment separately like the following.

```
$ flatpak run --command='sh' org.gnome.Polari
$ gsettings set org.gtk.Settings.Debug enable-
inspector-keybinding true.
```

GUI Designers

There are many GUI designers for GTK. The given projects are active as of July 2011 as follows:

Glade Interface Designer

It is a GUI builder for GTK, with additional components for GNOME. Glade Interface is a visual user interface builder for GTK, with different components for GNOME. It supports GtkBuilder, which is a GTK built-in GUI description format.

- Gazpacho is a GUI builder for the GTK toolkit written in Python
- Crow Designer relies on its GuiXml format and GuiLoader library
- Stetic is a part of MonoDevelop, oriented toward Gtk#

- Gambas since version 2.0 atop BASIC

- Xojo on Linux

- Lazarus on Linux defaults to interfacing with GTK 2

GtkBuilder

It allows user interfaces to be designed without writing code. The interface is described in an Extensible Markup Language (XML) file, loaded at runtime, and the objects are created automatically. The Glade Interface Designer allows creating the user interface in a what you see is what you get (WYSIWYG) manner. The user interface description is independent of the programming language being used.

Language Binding

Binding is an application programming interface (API) that provides glue code to allow a programming language to use a foreign library or operating system service.

LIST OF LANGUAGE BINDINGS FOR GTK

GTK supports a wide range of bindings for various languages that implement most of its feature set, whereas GTK 2 is no longer supported, meaning some languages discussed below do not have current GTK support.

- GObject was initially written as a main component of GTK but outsourced into GLib.

- GObject Introspection is a middleware layer between C libraries (using GObject) and language bindings, e.g., PyGObject uses this, while PyGTK does not.

- Official GNOME Bindings follow the GNOME release schedule, guaranteeing API stability and time-based releases.

- Glade Interface Designer.

List of Languages

- Ada

- C

- C#

- C#

- C++

- Crystal

- Crystal

- D

- Erlang

- Fortran

- FreeBASIC

- Gambas

- Genie

- Go

- Go

- Guile

- Haskell

- J

- Java and other JVM languages

- JavaScript   Gjs

- JavaScript   Seed

- Julia   Gtk.jl

- Kotlin/Native

- Lua

- Nim

- Objective-C

- OCaml

- ooRexx

- Pascal

- Perl

- PHP

- Prolog

- Python

- R

- Ruby

- Rust

- Smalltalk

- Standard ML

- Tcl

- Vala

- Wrapl

DESKTOP ENVIRONMENTS BASED ON GTK

Desktop environments that use GTK.

A desktop environment implements the desktop metaphor of a bundle of programs running on top of an operating system that shares a standard GUI, sometimes described as a graphical shell.

A desktop environment consists of icons, windows, toolbars, folders, wallpapers, and desktop widgets. A GUI also provides drag and drop and other features that make the complete desktop metaphor. A desktop environment aims to be an intuitive way for the user to interact with the computer using concepts similar to those used when interacting with the physical world such as buttons and windows.

While the desktop environment originally described a style of user interfaces following the desktop metaphor, it also represents the programs that realize the metaphor itself. The usage has been popularized by projects such as the Common Desktop Environment, K Desktop Environment, and GNOME.

Implementation

The window manager supports the user interactions with the environment, where the toolkit provides developers a software library for applications with a unified look and behavior.

A windowing system generally interfaces directly with the underlying operating system and libraries. It provides support for graphical hardware, pointing devices, and keyboards. The window manager typically runs on top of this windowing system. While the windowing system may give some window management functionality, this functionality is still considered part of the window manager, which happens to have been provided by the windowing system. A windowing toolkit provides applications access to widgets that allow users to interact graphically with the application consistently.

History of the GUI

The desktop environment was created by Xerox and sold with Xerox Alto in the 1970s. Xerox generally considered the Alto a personal office computer; it failed in the marketplace because of poor marketing and a very high price tag. Apple introduced a desktop environment on an affordable personal computer with the Lisa, failing in the market.

In 2014, the most popular desktop environments were the successor of these earlier environments, including the Windows shell operated in Microsoft Windows and the Aqua environment in macOS. Compared with the X-based environments available for Unix-like systems, such as Linux and FreeBSD, the proprietary desktop environments included with Windows and macOS have relatively fixed layouts and static features, with highly integrated "seamless" designs that aim to provide primarily consistent customer experiences across installations.

Microsoft Windows dominates in market share among computers with a desktop environment. Systems using Unix-like operating systems such as macOS, Chrome OS, Linux, BSD, or Solaris, are much less common. As of 2015, there is a growing market for low-cost Linux PCs using the X Window System or Wayland with a broad choice of desktop environments. Among the more popular are Google's Chromebooks and Chromeboxes, Intel's NUC, the Raspberry Pi, etc.

The situation is the opposite on tablets and smartphones, with Unix-like operating systems dominating the market, including iOS, Android, Tizen, Sailfish, and Ubuntu. Microsoft's Windows Phone and RT 10 are used on a much smaller number of tablets and smartphones. However, most Unix-like operating systems dominant on handheld devices do not use the X11 desktop environments used by other Unix-like operating systems, relying instead on interfaces based on different technologies.

Examples of Desktop Environments

The most common desktop environment on the system is Windows Shell in Microsoft Windows. Microsoft has made efforts in making Windows shell. As a result, Microsoft has introduced theme in Windows version 98, the various Windows XP visual styles, the Aero brand in Windows Vista, the Microsoft design language in Windows 8, Windows Spotlight in Windows 10. Its shell can be extended via Shell extensions.

The desktop environments for Unix-like operating systems use the X Window System, including KDE, GNOME, Xfce, LXDE, and Aqua, which users may select and are not tied exclusively to the operating system in use.

Several other desktop environments also exist, including CDE, EDE, GEM, IRIX Interactive Desktop, Sun's Java Desktop System, Jesktop, Mezzo, ROX Desktop, UDE, Xito, and many.

X window managers meant to be usable stand-alone – without another desktop environment also include elements of those found in typical desktop environments, most prominently Enlightenment. Other examples include OpenBox, Fluxbox, WindowLab, Fvwm, WindowMaker, and AfterStep, which feature the NeXTSTEP GUI look feel. However, new versions of operating systems make them configured.

- Ambient

- Bugie Desktop

- Budgie

- CDE

- Cinnamon

- Cutefish

- Deepin DE

- EDE

- Elokab

- Enlightenment

- Étoilé

- GNOME Shell

- GNUstep
- Innova
- Katana
- KDE Plasma 5
- Liri Shell
- Lumina
- LXDE
- LXQt
- MATE
- MaXX
- Maynard
- Mezzo
- Moksha
- Pantheon
- Project Looking Glass
- oZone GUI
- Razor-qt
- ROX Desktop
- Sugar
- theShell
- Trinity
- UKUI (desktop environment)
- Unity
- vera
- Xfce

Gtk#

It is a set of .NET Framework bindings for the GTK GUI toolkit and various GNOME libraries. The library facilitates building graphical GNOME applications using Mono or other compliant Common Language Runtime (CLR). It is an event-driven system like any other modern windowing library where every widget allows associating handler methods, which get called when certain events occur.

Applications built using Gtk# will run on various platforms, including Linux, Windows, and macOS. The Mono packages for Windows include GTK, Gtk#, a native theme to make applications look like native Windows applications. Running Gtk# applications on macOS no longer requires running an X11 server.

Glade Interface Designer is used with the Glade# bindings to design GUI applications easily. A GUI designer, "Stetic," is integrated with the MonoDevelop integrated development environment (IDE).

In addition, to support the standard GTK-GNOME development tools, the gtk-dotnet.dll provides a bridge to consume functionality on the .NET stack.

It supports Gtk3 and forked projects such as GtkSharp, founded to provide full Gtk3 support for C# and various CLI languages.

GTK is developed by The GNOME Project, which develops the GNOME Development Platform and the GNOME Desktop Environment.

GTK development is loosely managed. GNOME developers and users gather at an annual GNOME Users And Developers European Conference (GUADEC) meeting to discuss GNOME's current state and future direction. GNOME incorporates standards and programs from site freedesktop.org to better interoperate with other desktops.

Desktop Environments of GTK

Several desktop environments uses GTK as the widget toolkit given below.

Current Version

GNOME is based on GTK, meaning that programs native to GNOME use GTK:

- Budgie is built from scratch for the SolusOS successor, Solus Operating System

- Cinnamon is a fork of GNOME 3 which uses GTK version 3

- MATE, a fork of GNOME 2 which used GTK 3 since version 1.18

- Xfce is based on GTK 3 since version 4.14

- Pantheon uses GTK 3, being developed by elementary OS

- Sugar is a desktop environment for primary education, which uses GTK is especially for PyGTK

- Phosh, a mobile UI designed for PureOS

- LXDE is based on GTK 2

- COSMIC, a GNOME fork developed by System76

Window Managers
The following window managers use GTK:

- Aewm

- AfterStep

- Amaterus

- Consortium

- IceWM

- Marco

- Metacity

- Muffin

- Mutter

- Sawfish

- Wmg

- Xfwm

GtkInspector
GtkInspector was introduced with version 3.14. It can be invoked after installing the development package libgtk-3-dev/gtk+-devel.

GtkBuilder
It allows user interfaces to be designed without writing code. The interface is described in an XML file, loaded at runtime, and the objects are created

automatically. The Glade Interface Designer allows creating the user interface in a WYSIWYG. The user interface description is independent of the programming language being used.

GtkSourceView

For syntax highlighting, there is GtkSourceView, the "source code editing widget." GtkSourceView is maintained by GNOME separately from GTK as a library: gtksourceview. There are plans to rename it to gsv.

GtkSpell

It is a library separate from GTK. It depends on GTK and Enchants. Enchant is used for ispell, hunspell, etc., the actual spell checker software. It uses GTK's GtkTextView widget to highlight misspelled words and replace them.

GTK+

GTK+ History

GTK+ was started as a toolkit for the GIMP around 1996 and reached its stable release in April 1998. GTK+ version 1.0 contained the basic widgets needed to support the GIMP. The next release, 1.2, February 1999, contained many new widgets, which made GTK+ a valuable toolkit to choose for general application development. It was no longer Gimp-centric. 1.2 was also the first release that featured a separate GLib library.

After version 1.2, GTK+ went into a long development cycle, during which many things were done, such as text rendering being moved to use Pango, yielding first-class internationalization support. The object system was generalized and moved to GLib under the name GObject. A backend separation was introduced in GDK, and the win32 backend was added. Two big new widgets, the text view and the tree view were created from scratch. Both feature a model-view architecture. GNOME eagerly waited for GTK+ 2.0 to get ready during these three years since GNOME 2.0 depended on it. One of the lessons the GTK+ team learned from the 2.0 release cycle is to stick to shorter 9 to 12-month development cycles between stable releases.

The releases after 2.0 had more of untouched nature. The main new feature in version 2.2 was multi-head support for traditional X11 multiscreen/multi-display and Xinerama. One exciting aspect of the multi-head support in GTK+ is that it allows you to move windows between screens and displays, a feature that only a few toolkits support today. The current stable release version 2.4 features a new, much-anticipated file chooser widget, a new combo box, and some devices "brought home" from other places in the GNOME library stack.

Introduction to GTK+

It is a library for creating GUIs. The library is made in the C programming language. The GTK+ library is also called the GIMP toolkit. Initially, the library was created while developing the GIMP image manipulation program. Since then, the GTK+ has become one of the most popular toolkits under Linux and BSD Unix. Today, most of the GUI software in the open-source world is created in Qt or GTK+. The GTK+ is an object-oriented API. The object-oriented system is made with the Glib Object system, a base for the GTK+ library. GObject also enables the creation of language bindings for various other programming languages. Language bindings exist for C++, Python, Perl, Java, C#, and other programming languages.

The GTK+ depends on the following libraries:

- Glib

- Pango

- ATK

- GDK

- GdkPixbuf

- Cairo

The Glib is a general-purpose utility library. It provides various data types, string utilities, enables error reporting, message logging, working with threads, and other helpful programming features. Pango is a library that allows internationalization. ATK is the accessibility toolkit; it provides tools that help physically challenged people to work with computers. GDK is a wrapper around the underlying graphics system's low-level drawing and windowing functions. On Linux, GDK lies between the X Server and the GTK+ library. It handles basic rendering such as drawing primitives, raster graphics, cursors, fonts, window events, and drag-and-drop functionality. The GdkPixbuf library is a toolkit for image loading and pixel buffer manipulation. Cairo is used for creating 2D vector graphics. It has been included in GTK+ since version 2.8.

GNOME and XFce desktop environments have been created using the GTK+ library. SWT and wxWidgets are well-known programming frameworks that use GTK+. Prominent software applications that use GTK+ include Firefox or Inkscape.

Compiling GTK+ Applications

To compile GTK+ applications, we have a tool called pkg-config – the pgk-config returns metadata about already installed libraries. If you want to use a particular library, it provides the necessary dependent libraries and includes required files. The pkg-config retrieves information about packages from particular metadata files.

```
$ gcc -o simple.c "pkg-config --libs --cflags
gtk+-2.0"
```

The line compiles a basic program. The source code consists of one file simple.c.

Current Goals of GTK+ Development

The long-term goal for developing GTK+ is to provide a complete platform for the development of GUI applications. To achieve this, we have to close some points. Some of the commonly used widgets are currently missing in GTK+ are:

- a model-view table widget

- an icon list, like the icon view seen in Nautilus and other file managers

- a dock widget as seen in IDEs

- a print dialog

- an about dialog

- the wizards

Implementations or prototypes for some of these widgets are already available somewhere in the GNOME library stack and need to be cleaned and moved to GTK+. For example, there is an icon list widget called EggIconList in libegg, and a dialog named GNOMEAbout in libgnomeui. In other cases, the available implementation will have to rework more thoroughly before going into GTK+. An example is the print dialog. While there is an implementation in libgnomeprintui, the plan for a print dialog in GTK+ is to move to Cairo as the main rendering API and use the print support in Cairo. There are several dock widgets available in various parts of the GNOME library stack, which need to be carefully compared to develop a reasonable scope and feature set for a GTK+ dock widget. The complication of this particular widget is that there may be several non-compatible sets of requirements for a dock widget, coming from the use cases of IDEs and office-style applications. Finally, some widgets have been written from scratch. An example of this is the model-view table widget, although it would be desirable to reuse parts of the tree view widget such as the cell renderers.

Beyond simply adding more widgets, you would expect some essential features in a modern toolkit, which are currently absent from GTK+. Among them are: support for session management loading widget hierarchies from textual descriptions, like libglade, does more flexible layout using width-for-height geometry management User interface design keeps changing. Current trends like breaking up the window metaphor, introducing transparency and animation throughout the UI will force GTK+ to evolve. We can achieve the goals while maintaining binary compatibility with GTK+ 2. x.

Installations

GTK is available on:

- GNU/Linux and Unix

- Windows

- Mac OS X

Instead, you can check out the latest release (unstable) of GTK using git.

```
$ git clone https://gitlab.gnome.org/GNOME/gtk.git
```

Installing GTK for GNU/Linux and Unix
To install GTK for GNU-Linux and other Unix systems, you need to get the GLib, GObject-Introspection, Pango, Gdk-Pixbuf, ATK, and GTK packages to build GTK.

Stable Version

To build an environment for GTK, you need to install all the dependencies listed as follows:

List of dependencies:

- GTK
- GLib
- Pango
- Gdk-pixbuf
- ATK
- GObject-Introspection
- Epoxy

And the current stable API version of GTK is 4.0.

Development Version

To build the development version of GTK, you can use a tool like JHBuild or rely on meson, which will download and create many dependencies as subprojects if they are not available on the system.

Older Versions

Still, many applications use GTK 3, an older version of GTK. You can also have the run-time and development environments for GTK 4.x and 3.x installed simultaneously on your system.

TABLE 4.1   Installing GTK from Packages

Distribution	Binary Package	Development Package	Additional Packages
Arch	gtk4	–	–
Debian/Ubuntu	libgtk-4-1	libgtk-4-dev	gtk-4-examples
Fedora	gtk4	gtk4-devel	–

TABLE 4.2   Installing GTK3 from Packages

Distribution	Binary Package	Development Package	Additional Packages
Arch	gtk3	–	–
Debian/Ubuntu	libgtk-3-0	libgtk-3-dev	gtk-3-examples
Fedora	gtk3	gtk3-devel	–

TABLE 4.3   Architecture of GTK+

Application			
GTK+			
ATK	Pango	Gdk-pixbug	GDK
Glib	Gmodule	GOject	Window System

To read more about these packages, you can refer to the Architecture as follow (see the following figure).

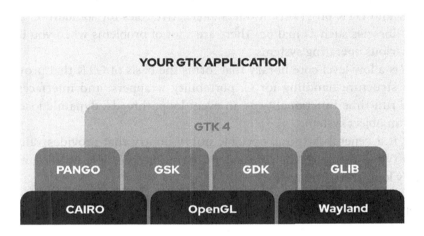

GTK Application.

- **Glib:** It provides low-level data structures, types, thread support, the event loop, and dynamic loading.

- **GObject:** It implements an object-oriented system in C without requiring C++.

- **Pango:** It supports text rendering and layout.

- **ATK (Accessibility ToolKit):** It helps you create accessible applications and allows users to run your applications with screen readers and other accessibility tools.

- **GDK (GIMP Drawing Kit):** It handles low-level graphics rendering on top of the Xlib.

- **GdkPixbuf:** It helps manipulate images within GTK+ programs.

- **Xlib:** It provides low-level graphics on Linux and UNIX systems.

- **GModule:** It is a portable method for dynamically loading "plug-ins."

After some time, GTK was built up to be based on various libraries developed by the GTK team.

These libraries are discussed here.

glib

It provides a series of functions and definitions useful when designing GDK and GTK programs. It offers alternative roles for standard C function libraries such as malloc. There are a lot of problems when you use it on various operating systems.

It is a low-level core library that forms the basis of GTK that provides data structure handling for C, portability wrappers, and interfaces for such run-time functionality as an event loop, threads, dynamic loading, and an object system.

It is a general-purpose, portable utility library that provides valuable data types, macros, type conversions, string utilities, file utilities, a primary loop abstraction, etc.

Dependencies with Descriptions:

- **GModule:** It is a portable API for dynamically loading modules.

- **GObject:** It is the base type system library.

- **GIO:** It is GObject Interfaces and Objects, Networking, IPC, and I/O.

GLib uses the Meson build system. The usual sequence for compiling and installing the GLib library is thus:

```
$ meson setup _build
$ meson compile -C _build
$ meson install -C _build
```

Before compiling the GLib library, you need to have other tools and libraries installed on the system. If you are creating from a release archive, you surely need a compliant C toolchain, Meson, and pkg-config. The requirements are the same when you build from a Git repository clone of GLib.

Dependencies:

- pkg-config is a tool for tracking the compilation flags needed for libraries used by the GLib library.

- A UNIX made of GLib requires that the system implements at least the original 1990 version of POSIX. Above this, it depends on several other libraries.

- The GNU libiconv library is needed to build GLib if your system doesn't have the iconv() conversion between character encodings. Most modern systems should have iconv(); however, many older systems lack an iconv() implementation. On such systems, you must install the libiconv library.

Pango

It is a library for the layout and rendering of text with an emphasis on internationalization. It forms the core of text and font handling for GTK.

Dependencies with descriptions

- **GObject:** The base type system library

- **HarfBuzz:** A text shaping library

- **PangoCairo:** Cairo support for Pango

- **PangoFc:** Fontconfig support for Pango

- **PangoFT2:** Freetype support for Pango

- **PangoOT:** OpenType support for Pango

- **PangoXft:** Xft support for Pango

Cairo

It is a library for 2D graphics with support for multiple output devices, including the X Window, Win32, while producing a constant output on all media while taking benefit of display hardware acceleration when available.

Its currently support output targets include the X Window System, Quartz, Win32, image buffers, PostScript, PDF, and SVG file output. Backends include OpenGL, BeOS, OS/2, and DirectFB.

Also, it is designed to produce consistent output on all output media while using display hardware acceleration when available (e.g., via the X Render Extension).

Its API provides operations similar to the graphic operators of PostScript and PDF. Operations in Cairo include:

- Stroking and filling cubic Bézier splines.

- Transforming and compositing translucent images.

- Antialiased text rendering.

Any affine transformation can change all drawing operations such as scale, rotation, shear, etc.

Cairo is implemented as a library written in the C programming language. The Bindings are available for several different programming languages. It is free software and can be redistributed and modified under the terms of either the GNU LGPL version 2.1 or the Mozilla Public License (MPL) version 1.1 at your option.

Language Bindings

A library that can be written in one programming language can also be used in another language if bindings are written; Cairo has a range of bindings for various languages, including C++, C#, and other CLI languages such as Delphi, Eiffel, Factor, Harbour, Haskell, Julia, Lua, Perl, PHP, Python, Ruby, Rust, Scheme, Smalltalk, and others like Gambas.

Toolkit Bindings

Since Cairo is a drawing library, it can be pretty helpful to integrate it with a GUI toolkit. GTK began in 2005, with version 2.8, to use Cairo to render most of its graphical control elements, and since version 3.0, all rendering is done through Cairo. The Cairo development team maintains up-to-date instructions for rendering surfaces to SDL.

Cairo supports output to several different back-ends, known as "surfaces" in its code. Back-ends support includes output to the X Window System via Xlib and XCB, Win32 GDI, OS X Quartz Compositor, the BeOS API, OS/2, OpenGL contexts, and local image buffers, PNG files, PDF, PostScript, DirectFB, and SVG files.

There are other back-ends in development targeting the graphics APIs OpenVG, Qt, Skia, and Microsoft's Direct2D.

Usage

Cairo is famous in the open-source community for providing cross-platform support for advanced 2D drawing.

- The Mono Project, including Moonlight, has been using Cairo since very early in conception to power the backends of its GDI+ (libgdiplus) and System. Drawing namespaces.

- The Mozilla project has used Cairo in its Gecko layout engine, used for rendering the graphical output of Mozilla products. Gecko 1.8, the layout engine for Mozilla Firefox 2.0 and SeaMonkey 1.0, used Cairo to render SVG and <canvas> content. Gecko 1.9, the release of Gecko that serves as the basis of Firefox 3, uses Cairo as the graphics backend for rendering web page content, and the user interface.

- The WebKit framework uses Cairo for all GTK and EFL ports rendering. Using Cairo, support has also been added for SVG and <canvas> content.

- The Poppler library uses Cairo to render PDF documents. Cairo enables the drawing of antialiased vector graphics and transparent objects.

- The vector graphics application Inkscape uses the Cairo library for its outline mode display and PDF and PostScript.

GdkPixbuf

GdkPixbuf is a library for graphical loading assets like icons in various formats, like PNG, JPEG, and GIF. GdkPixbuf is a library that loads image data in multiple formats and stores it as linear buffers in memory. The buffers can be scaled, composited, modified, saved, or rendered. It can load image data encoded in different formats, such as:

- PNG

- JPEG

- TIFF

- TGA

- GIF

Additionally, you can write a GdkPixbuf-loader module and install it into a prominent location to load a file format. The GTK toolkit uses GdkPixbuf for loading graphical assets.

Building GdkPixbuf

Requirements: To build GdkPixbuf, you will also need to have installed:

- A C99-compliant compiler and toolchain

- Meson

- Glib's development files

Depending on the image formats you like to support, you will need, libpng's, libjpeg's, libtiff's development files.

Additionally, you may need:

- shared-mime-info

- GObject Introspection

- GI-DocGen

- mediaLib's development files

Installing GdkPixbuf

You can use Meson to configure GdkPixbuf's build. Depending on the platform, you will use Ninja, Visual Studio, or XCode to build the project; generally, on most media, you should be able to use the following commands to build and install GdkPixbuf in the default prefix:

```
$ meson setup _build.
$ Meson compile -C _build
$ Meson install -C _build
```

You can use Meson's as --prefix argument to control the installation prefix at configuration time. You can use Meson configure from within the build directory to check the current build configuration, and change its options.

Build Options

We can have the following options in the command line to meson:

- **-Dgtk_doc=true:** Build the API reference documentation

- **-Drelocatable=true:** Enable application bundle relocation support

ATK

Accessibility Toolkit (ATK) is an open-source software library, part of the GNOME project, which provides APIs for implementing accessibility support in software.

One standard nomenclature to explain an accessibility framework is a usual client-server architecture. In that way, assistive technologies (ATs) as screen readers can be the clients of that framework, and computer applications would be the server. In the architecture, the client and server need to communicate with each other, usually using the IPC technology of the platform.

Usually, the API for both client and server-side applications are the same, and the accessibility framework provides a client and server-side implementation of that API. In GNOME, there are two types of APIs, one for the client-side (Assistive Technology Service Provider Interface (AT-SPI)) and a different one for the server-side (ATK) due to historical reasons related to the underlying technologies.

Implementations

The ATK abstract headers files are available to help developers make their GUI toolkit accessible. Developers who use stock widgets of GUI toolkits that implement the ATK headers. However, if they develop their widgets, they will have to ensure that they expose all the accessible information.

GNOME Accessibility Implementation Library (GAIL) was the name of the accessibility interfaces implementation-defined by ATK for GTK+, the widget library of GNOME. Initially, it was an independent module mapped to GTK+, while since GNOME 3.2, GAIL was merged into GTK+, the ATK implementation is integrated into GTK+, and GAIL is deprecated.

Apart from GTK+, other GUI toolkits and applications have implemented ATK to be accessible such as OpenOffice-LibreOffice, Mozilla's Gecko, Clutter, and WebKitGTK+.

Repository Browser

You can also download the dependencies from their git repository from your web browser for gtk, glib, pango, gdk-pixbuf, and atk.

CREATE GUI IN GTK TOOLKIT

In many programming languages, GUI improvement is one of its languages highlights centerpieces. Still, C has no such library connected to it like the string library, IO library, etc., that we now and again use. This weakness opened the skyline for engineers to pick from a wide assortment of GUI library toolbox accessible in C. GTK+ is one of them. It represents GIMP Toolkit and can program current GUI interfaces.

The helpful thing about GTK+ is that it is controlled, developed, and its starting point can be followed back to the past times of X Windows that structure the center GUI arrangement of Linux today. GTK is written entirely in C, and the GTK+ programming that we regularly use in Linux is also in C. For example, the work area administrators, GNOME and XFCE, are likewise manufactured utilizing GTK.

A GTK+ application isn't limited to the Linux stage anyone, but; it very well may be ported to non-UNIX/Linux steps also.

Here, we will cling to the primary type of GTK+, its C avatar on the Linux stage. The official webpage to download GTK+ is https://www.gtk. org. The site contains API documentation, instructional exercises, and other GNOME libraries frequently utilized alongside GTK. GTK is based on libraries, for example,

- **ATK:** This library provides help to create accessibility tools such as sticky keys, screen readers, etc.

- **Glib:** It is a universally helpful utility library that offers help for threads, dynamic loading, event loops, low-level data structures, etc.

- **GObject:** This library gives C full-featured object-oriented help without C++. This library encourages the language binding made for different languages to provide you with simple access to C APIs.

- **GdkPixBuf:** This library gives picture control capacities.

- **GDK (GIMP Drawing Toolkit):** This design library gives low-level drawing capacities over Xlib.

- **Pango:** This library helps in content and design rendering
- **Xlib:** This library provides low-level graphics support for the Linux system.

When composing code with GTK, we locate that a significant number of the primitive data types are prefixed with "g" as in

- gint
- gchar
- gshort
- gpointer

GLib defines several commonly used types, which can be divided into four groups:

The new types which are not part of standard C – gboolean, gsize, gssize.

- Integer types are guaranteed to be the same size across all platforms – gint8, guint8, gint16, guint16, gint32, guint32, gint64, and guint64.
- Types that are easier to use than their standard C counterparts are gpointer, gconstpointer, guchar, guint, gushort, and gulong.
- Types that correspond exactly to standard C types but are included for completeness are gchar, gint, gshort, glong, gfloat, and gdouble.

Details of data type:

- gboolean
  typedef gint gboolean;
      It is a standard boolean type where type variables should contain the value TRUE or FALSE.

- gpointer
  typedef void* gpointer;
      It is an untyped pointer where gpointer looks better and is easier to use than void*.

- gconstpointer
  typedef const void *gconstpointer;
      It is an untyped pointer to constant data and pointed data should not be changed.

- gchar
  typedef char gchar;
    It corresponds to the standard C char type.

- guchar
  typedef unsigned char guchar;
    It corresponds to the standard C unsigned char type.

- gint
  typedef int gint;
    It corresponds to the standard C int type.

- guint
  typedef unsigned int guint;
    It corresponds to the standard C unsigned int type.

- gshort
  typedef short gshort;
    It corresponds to the standard C short type.

- gushort
  typedef unsigned short gushort;
    It corresponds to the standard C unsigned short type.

- glong
  typedef long glong;
    It corresponds to the standard C long type.

- gulong
  typedef unsigned long gulong;
    It corresponds to the standard C unsigned long type.

- gint8

- typedef signed char gint8;
  It is a signed integer guaranteed to be 8 bits on all platforms.

- guint8
  typedef unsigned char guint8;
    It is an unsigned integer guaranteed to be 8 bits on all platforms.

- gint16
  typedef signed short gint16;
    It is a signed integer guaranteed to be 16 bits on all platforms.
  Values of this type can range from -32,768 to 32,767.

- guint16

  typedef unsigned short guint16;

     It is an unsigned integer guaranteed to be 16 bits on all platforms. Values of this type can range from 0 to 65,535.

- gint32

  typedef signed int gint32;

     A signed integer is guaranteed to be 32 bits on all platforms. Values of this type can range from -2,147,483,648 to 2,147,483,647.

- guint32

  typedef unsigned int guint32;

     An unsigned integer is guaranteed to be 32 bits on all platforms. Values of this type can range from 0 to 4,294,967,295.

- G_HAVE_GINT64

  #define G_HAVE_GINT64 1 /* deprecated, always true */

     It is defined if 64-bit signed and unsigned integers are available on the platform.

- gint64

  G_GNUC_EXTENSION typedef signed long, long gint64;

     It is a signed integer guaranteed to be 64 bits on all platforms. Range lies between -9,223,372,036,854,775,808 and 9,223,372,036, 854,775,807.

- guint64

  G_GNUC_EXTENSION typedef unsigned long long guint64;

     It is an unsigned integer guaranteed to be 64 bits on all platforms. Values of range from 0 to 18,446,744,073,709,551,615.

- gfloat

  typedef float gfloat;

     It corresponds to the standard C float type.

- gdouble

  typedef double gdouble;

     It corresponds to the standard C double type.

- gsize

  typedef unsigned int gsize;

     It is an unsigned 32-bit integer intended to represent sizes of data structures.

- gssize
  typedef signed int gssize;
  It is a signed 32-bit integer intended to represent sizes of data structures.

These types guarantee that the code can be used on any platform without rolling out any improvements. These types are characterized in these libraries to help make them platform-independent.

GUI programming has object-oriented in it, which is the main issue. In this, a procedural does not fit in this scheme. Therefore, regardless of GTK being written in C, it gives object-oriented help through GObject. Note that this item arranged service has nothing to do with C++. C++ has its GTK library, called gtkmm. GObject encourages a portion of the object-oriented principles, similar to polymorphism and inheritance, with the assistance of macros. The following figure illustrates the hierarchical relation.

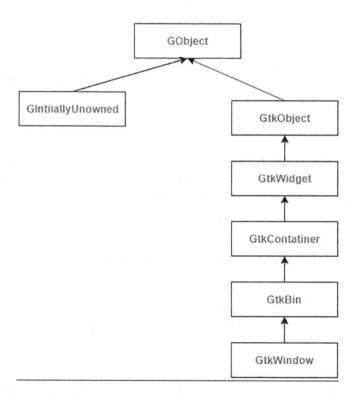

GObject hierarchical relation.

GtkWindow inherits the GtkBin, which is a child of GtkContainer. An object of GtkWindow can call the function defined in GtkBin or GtkContainer.

```
abstract class Gtk.Bin : Gtk.Container {
  container: GtkContainer
}
```

GtkBin

The GtkBin is a container with just one child. It is not very useful, but it helps derive subclasses since it provides standard code for handling a single child widget.

Many of the GTK+ widgets are subclasses of GtkBin, including GtkWindow, GtkButton, GtkFrame, GtkHandleBox, or GtkScrolledWindow.

Ancestors of GtkBin:

1. GtkContainer

2. GtkWidget

3. GInitiallyUnowned

4. GObject

Let's discuss all the above one by one,

GtkContainer

```
abstract class Gtk.Container : Gtk.Widget {
  widget: GtkWidget
}
```

Nesting widgets inside widgets construct a GTK+ user interface. Container widgets are the inner nodes in the tree of widgets and they can also contain other widgets. So, for example, you might have a GtkWindow containing a GtkFrame containing a GtkLabel. If you wanted an image instead of a textual label inside the frame, you might replace the GtkLabel widget with a GtkImage widget.

GtkWidget

There are two significant kinds of container widgets in GTK+. Both are subclasses of the abstract GtkContainer base class.

The first type of container widget has a single child widget and derives from GtkBin. These containers are decorators, which add functionality to the child. For example, a GtkButton makes its child into a clickable button; a GtkFrame draws a frame around its child, and a GtkWindow places its child widget inside a top-level window.

```
abstract class Gtk.Widget : GObject.InitiallyUnowned {
  parent_instance: GInitiallyUnowned
}
```

It is the base class all widgets in GTK+ derive from and manages the widget lifecycle, states, and style.

GInitiallyUnowned

```
class GObject.InitiallyUnowned : GObject.Object {
  g_type_instance: GTypeInstance
}
```

A type for objects that have an floating reference. All the fields in the GInitiallyUnowned structure are private to the implementation and should never be accessed directly.

```
class GObject.Object : GObject.TypeInstance {
  g_type_instance: GTypeInstance
}
```

The base object type.

```
class GObject.Object : GObject.TypeInstance {
  g_type_instance: GTypeInstance
}
```

All the fields in the above structure are private to the implementation.
Descendants of GInitiallyUnowned:

1. GBinding

2. GInitiallyUnowned

3. GTypeModule

Descendants of GtkBin:

1. GtkActionBar

2. GtkAlignment

3. GtkButton

4. GtkComboBox

5. GtkEventBox

6. GtkExpander

7. GtkFlowBoxChild

8. GtkFrame

9. GtkHandleBox

10. GtkListBoxRow

11. GtkMenuItem

12. GtkOverlay

13. GtkPopover

14. GtkRevealer

15. GtkScrolledWindow

16. GtkSearchBar

17. GtkStackSidebar

18. GtkToolItem

19. GtkViewport

20. GtkWindow

List Widgets

The GtkList widget is created to act as a vertical container for widgets of GtkListItem.

A GtkList widget has a window to receive events, and its background color is usually white. It is directly derived from a GtkContainer, and it can be treated as such by using the GTK_CONTAINER(List) macro; see the

GtkContainer widget for more details on this. One should already be familiar with using a GList and its related functions g_list_*() to use the GtkList widget to its full extent.

There is a field inside the structure definition of the GtkList widget that will greater interest to us, this is:

```
struct _GtkList
{
  [...]
  GList *selection;
  guint selection_mode;
  [...]
};
```

The selection field of a GtkList to a linked list of all currently selected items, or "NULL" if the selection is empty.

The selection_mode of the GtkList specifies the selection facilities of a GtkList and the contents of the GTK_LIST()->selection field:

The selection_mode can be one of the following:

- GTK_SELECTION_SINGLE
  It is either "NULL" or contains a GList* pointer for a single selected item.

- GTK_SELECTION_BROWSE
  It is "NULL" if the list contains no widgets or insensitive ones only; otherwise, it includes a GList pointer for one GList structure and, therefore, exactly one list item.

- GTK_SELECTION_MULTIPLE
  It is "NULL" if no list items are selected or a GList pointer for the first selected item.

- GTK_SELECTION_EXTENDED
  It is always "NULL." The default is GTK_SELECTION_MULTIPLE.

GTK+ Widgets

These are the building blocks of a GUI application. Over the years, several widgets became a standard in programming toolkits, for example, a button, a check box, or a scroll bar. The GTK+ toolkit's philosophy is to keep the number of widgets at a minimum level. More specialized widgets are created as custom GTK+ widgets.

1. **GtkLabel**

```
final class Gtk.Label : Gtk.Widget {
  /* No available fields */
}
```

The GtkLabel displays a small amount of text, but most labels label another widget such as a GtkButton.

2. **GtkSpinner**

```
final class Gtk.Spinner : Gtk.Widget {
  /* other fields */
}
```

A GtkSpinner displays an icon-size spinning animation, and it is often used as an alternative to a GtkProgressBar for displaying indefinite activity instead of actual progress.

An example GtkSpinner, to start the animation, use gtk_spinner_start(), to stop it use gtk_spinner_stop().

3. **GtkStatusbar**

```
final class Gtk.Statusbar : Gtk.Widget {
  /* other fields */
}
```

A GtkStatusbar is placed along the bottom of an application's main GtkWindow. A GtkStatusBar may provide a regular commentary of the application's status. status bars in GTK maintain a stack of messages. The message at the top of each bar's stack is the one that will currently be displayed.

4. **GtkImage**

```
final class Gtk.Image : Gtk.Widget {
  /* other fields */
}
```

The GtkImage widget displays an image.

An example, the various kinds of object can be displayed as an image; you can load a GdkTexture from a file, using the function gtk_image_new_from_file(), for example:

```
GtkWidget *image = gtk_image_new_from_file ("my_
file.png");
```

5. **GtkTextView**

```
class Gtk.TextView : Gtk.Widget {
  parent_instance: GtkWidget
}
```

A widget displays the contents of a GtkTextBuffer.

An example GtkTextview

You may begin by reading the conceptual overview, which explains all the objects and data types related to the text widget and how they work together.

6. **GtkMediaControls**

```
final class Gtk.MediaControls : Gtk.Widget {
  /* other fields */
}
```

GtkMediaControls is used to show controls for a video. Usually, it is used as part of GtkVideo.

7. **GtkCalendar**

```
final class Gtk.Calendar : Gtk.Widget {
  /* other fields */
}
```

GtkCalendar displays a Gregorian calendar, one month at a time.

An example GtkCalendar

A GtkCalendar can create with gtk_calendar_new().

The date is currently displayed can be altered with gtk_calendar_select_day(). To place a marker on a particular day, use gtk_calendar_mark_day() and to remove the marker, gtk_calendar_unmark_day(). Alternative, all marks can clear with gtk_calendar_clear_marks(). The selected date can retrieve from a GtkCalendar using gtk_calendar_get_date().

8. **GtkWindowControls**

```
final class Gtk.WindowControls : Gtk.Widget {
  /* other fields */
}
```

GtkWindowControls shows window frame controls.

Typical window frame controls are minimized, maximize, and close buttons, and the window icon. An example GtkWindowControls, it only displays the start or end side of the controls, so it's intended to be continuously used in pair with another GtkWindowControls for the opposite side.

Other Display Widgets:

- **GtkAccelLabel:** A label that displays an accelerator key on the right of the text

- **GtkImage:** A widget displaying an image

- **GtkLabel:** A widget displays a small to medium amount of text

- **GtkProgressBar:** A widget that indicates progress visually

- **GtkStatusbar:** Report messages of minor importance to the user

- **GtkInfoBar:** Report essential messages to the user

- **GtkStatusIcon:** It displays an icon in the system tray

- **GtkSpinner:** It shows a spinner animation

9. **GtkButton**

```
class Gtk.Button : Gtk.Widget {
  /*  other fields */
}
```

The GtkButton widget triggers a callback function when the button is pressed. An example GtkButton widget can hold any valid child widget. It can hold almost any other standard GtkWidget. The most commonly used child is the GtkLabel.

10. **GtkCheckButton**

```
class Gtk.CheckButton : Gtk.Widget {
  parent_instance: GtkWidget
}
```

A GtkCheckButton can places a label next to an indicator using calling gtk_check_button_new() or gtk_check_button_new_with_label().

The state of a GtkCheckButton can set using gtk_check_button_set_active(), and retrieved using gtk_check_button_get_active().

11. **GtkCheckButton**

```
class Gtk.CheckButton : Gtk.Widget {
  parent_instance: GtkWidget
}
```

A GtkCheckButton places a label next to an indicator and created by calling either gtk_check_button_new() or gtk_check_button_new_with_label().

The state of a GtkCheckButton can be set specifically using gtk_check_button_set_active(), and retrieved using gtk_check_button_get_active().

12. **GtkComboBox**

```
class Gtk.ComboBox : Gtk.Widget {
  parent_instance: GtkWidget
}
```

A GtkComboBox widget allows the user to choose from a list of valid choices and displays the selected option; when activated, it shows a popup that allows the user to make a new choice.

It uses the model-view pattern; the list of valid choices is specified in a tree model. The display of the options can be adapted to the data in the model by using cell renderers, as you would in a tree view since it implements the GtkCellLayout interface.

To allow the user to enter values not in the model, the GtkComboBox: The has-entry property allows the GtkComboBox to contain a GtkEntry. This entry can access by calling gtk_combo_box_get_child() on the combo box.

13. **GtkColorButton**

```
final class Gtk.ColorButton : Gtk.Widget {
  /* other fields */
}
```

The GtkColorButton allows you to open a color chooser dialog to change the color.

It is a suitable widget for selecting a color in a preference dialog.

14. **GtkSearchEntry**

```
final class Gtk.SearchEntry : Gtk.Widget {
  /* other fields */
}
```

GtkSearchEntry is an entry widget used as a search entry. The main API for interacting with a GtkSearchEntry as entry is the GtkEditable interface. It will show an idle symbolic "find" icon when the search entry is empty and an extended "clear" icon when there is text. Clicking on the "clear" icon will empty the search entry.

15. **GtkSpinButton**

```
final class Gtk.SpinButton : Gtk.Widget {
  /* other  fields */
}
```

A GtkSpinButton is a way to allow the user to set the value of some attribute. It will enable the user to click on two arrows to increment or decrement the displayed value. The main properties of a GtkSpinButton are through an adjustment.

Buttons and Toggles

- **GtkButton:** Creates a signal when you click on

- **GtkCheckButton:** Creates widgets with a discrete toggle button

- **GtkRadioButton:** A choice from multiple check buttons

- **GtkToggleButton:** Creates buttons that retain their state

- **GtkLinkButton:** Creates buttons bound to a URL

- **GtkScaleButton:** A button that pops up a scale

- **GtkVolumeButton:** A button that pops up a volume control

- **GtkSwitch:** A "light switch" style toggle

Other Numeric/Text Data Entry

- **GtkEntry:** A single-line text entry field. The GtkEntry widget is a single-line text entry widget. An extensive set of key bindings are supported by default. When you enter passwords and other sensitive information, it can be put into "password mode" using gtk_entry_set_visibility().

- **GtkEntryBuffer:** Text buffer for GtkEntry. The GtkEntryBuffer class contains the exact text displayed in a GtkEntry widget. A single GtkEntryBuffer object can share by multiple GtkEntry widgets, which will transfer the same text content, but not the cursor position, visibility attributes, icon, etc.

- **GtkEntryCompletion:** Completion functionality for GtkEntry. GtkEntryCompletion is an object used in conjunction with GtkEntry to provide complete functionality. It implements the GtkCellLayout interface to allow the user to add extra cells to the GtkTreeView with completion matches.

- **GtkScale:** It is the base class for GtkHScale and GtkVScale.

- **GtkHScale:** It is a horizontal slider widget for selecting a value from a range.

- **GtkVScale:** It is a vertical slider widget for selecting a value from a range.

- **GtkSpinButton:** It retrieves an integer or floating-point number from the user. A GtkSpinButton allows the user to set the value of some attribute. It enables the user to click on one of two arrows to increment or decrement the displayed value.

- **GtkEditable:** Interface for text-editing widgets. The GtkEditable interface should be implemented by text editing widgets such as GtkEntry and GtkText. It contains functions for manipulating an editable widget, a large number of action signals used for key bindings, and other signals that an application can connect to modify the behavior of a widget.

Menus, Combo Box, Toolbar

- **GtkComboBox:** Used to choose from a list of items

- **GtkComboBoxText:** A simple, text-only combo box

- **GtkMenu:** A menu widget

- **GtkMenuBar:** A subclass of GtkMenuShell which holds GtkMenuItem widgets

- **GtkMenuItem:** The widget used for items in menus

- **GtkImageMenuItem:** A menu item with an icon

- **GtkRadioMenuItem:** A choice from multiple check menu items

- **GtkCheckMenuItem:** A item with a check box

- **GtkSeparatorMenuItem:** A separator used in menus

- **GtkTearoffMenuItem:** A menu item used to tear off and reattach its menu

- **GtkToolShell:** Interface for containers containing GtkToolItem widgets

- **GtkToolbar:** Creates bars of buttons and other widgets

- **GtkToolItem:** The base class of widgets that add to GtkToolShell

- **GtkToolPalette:** A tool palette with categories

- **GtkToolItemGroup:** A sub-container used in a tool palette

- **GtkSeparatorToolItem:** A toolbar item that separates groups of other toolbar items

- **GtkToolButton:** A GtkToolItem subclass that displays buttons

- **GtkMenuToolButton:** A GtkToolItem containing a button with an additional dropdown menu

- **GtkToggleToolButton:** A GtkToolItem having a toggle button

- **GtkRadioToolButton:** A toolbar item that includes a radio button

16. GtkGrid

```
class Gtk.Grid : Gtk.Widget {
  /* No available fields */
}
```

GtkGrid is a container that arranges its child widgets in rows and columns. It supports arbitrary positions and horizontal-vertical spans.

Their children are add using gtk_grid_attach(). They can span multiple rows or columns. It is possible to add a child next to an existing child, using gtk_grid_attach_next_to() and to remove a child from the grid, use gtk_grid_remove().

17. **GtkBox**

```
class Gtk.Box : Gtk.Widget {
  parent_instance: GtkWidget
}
```

The GtkBox widget sets child widgets into a single row or column.

Whether it is a row or a column depends on the value of GtkOrientable: orientation property. Within the dimension, all children are allocated the same size. Of course, the GtkWidget:halign and GtkWidget:valign properties can be used on the children to influence their allocation.

Layout Containers

- **GtkGrid:** Packs widgets in rows and columns

- **GtkAlignment:** A widget that controls the alignment and size of its child

- **GtkAspectFrame:** A-frame constrains its child to a particular aspect ratio

- **GtkBox:** Base class for box containers

- **GtkHBox:** A horizontal container box

- **GtkVBox:** A vertical container box

- **GtkButtonBox:** Base class for GtkHButtonBox and GtkVButtonBox

- **GtkHButtonBox:** A container for arranging buttons horizontally

- **GtkVButtonBox:** A container for organizing buttons vertically

- **GtkFixed:** A container that allows you to position widgets at fixed coordinates

- **GtkPaned:** Base class for widgets with two adjustable panes

- **GtkHPaned:** A container with two panes arranged horizontally

- **GtkVPaned:** A container with two panes set vertically

- **GtkLayout:** Infinite scrollable area containing child widgets and custom drawing

- **GtkNotebook:** A tabbed notebook container

- **GtkTable:** Pack widgets in regular patterns

- **GtkExpander:** A container that can hide its child

- **GtkOrientable:** An interface for flippable widgets

18. **GtkPaned**

```
final class Gtk.Paned : Gtk.Widget {
  /* No available fields */
}
```

GtkPaned has two panes that can be arranged either horizontally or vertically.

The user adjusts the division between the two panes by dragging a handle.

CHAPTER SUMMARY

In this chapter, we have learned in detail about the fundamentals of GTK programming, its software architecture, and GTK+, the updated version of GTK.

CHAPTER 5

Best GNOME-Based Linux Distros

IN THIS CHAPTER

➢ Ubuntu and DEB family GNOME-based Linux Distros

➢ Ubuntu and DEB family

➢ Fedora and RPM-based

➢ Zorin OS

➢ Linux Mint Cinnamon

➢ Debian testing

➢ Elementary OS

➢ Arch Linux

➢ OpenSUSE

➢ Solus

➢ Manjaro Gnome edition

In this chapter, we have covered GTK toolkit basic, and GNOME is a desktop environment that uses GTK+ as its GUI toolkit. It stands for GIMP Toolkit. It is first used to create design a user interface (UI) for GIMP.

DOI: 10.1201/9781003311942-5

Now, we will be going to cover various GNOME-based distros. GNOME3 is the default desktop environment on different major Linux distributions, including Fedora Linux, Rocky Linux, Red Hat Enterprise, Debian, Ubuntu, SUSE Linux Enterprise, CentOS, Pop!_OS, Oracle Linux, Endless OS, and Tails; as well as Solaris, a Unix operating system (OS).

Despite being the most widely used desktop environment, some Linux distros offer a better implementation of GNOME. Remember, we can put together a list of the best GNOME-based Linux distros on the market.

UBUNTU AND DEB FAMILY

It is a Debian-based Linux distribution popular among the Linux community. It's the first distro recommended to newcomers wanting to try out Linux. One of the most significant advantages of using Ubuntu is that soon there will be professional apps from big companies like Adobe, Microsoft, etc. (m47ade possible with snap). It is so eliminating the divide between users and prosumers. Ubuntu featured GNOME desktop last year, but slightly modified from the original one. The customized looks similar to the Unity desktop to ease the migration for old users. Still, the desktop seems refreshing, considering the developers have done a great job with themes and icons.

Installation of the GNOME

- Open a Terminal application on the Ubuntu system. Click the Dash icon on the top left and select Terminal from the app list to open the Terminal.

- You can also use Ctrl + Alt + T keyboard shortcuts to open the Terminal.

- Type $sudo apt-get update in Terminal window. The command will update all your repositories and ensure you have the latest versions of packages.

- Press ↵ Enter or ⏎ Return on your keyboard. It will run your command and update your repositories.

- If prompted, enter your admin user password and press ↵ Enter or ⏎ Return to proceed.

- Type sudo apt-get install ubuntu-GNOME-desktop. This command will install the complete GNOME desktop environment with the standard applications and optimizations for Ubuntu.

- Alternatively, you can install the GNOME Shell using the $sudo apt-get install GNOME-shell command.

- GNOME Shell installs the minimal packages required for the GNOME desktop environment, excluding the additional desktop apps and Ubuntu themes that come with the complete installation.

- The ubuntu-GNOME-desktop install includes GNOME Shell in it. Make sure you combine the two commands and type sudo apt-get install GNOME-shell ubuntu-GNOME-desktop.

- Press ↵ Enter on your keyboard. It will run the command and start installing the GNOME desktop environment on your computer.

- Enter y on your keyboard when they ask you. During the installation, you will get a prompt to upgrade several packages. Type y and hit Enter to proceed with the install.

- Then, select a display manager when asked. You can choose between GNOME, GNOME Classic, Ubuntu Wayland, Ubuntu as GNOME display manager at the end of the installation.

- GNOME is the default GNOME3 desktop environment greeter, and GNOME Classic is a GNOME Shell feature and mode for users who prefer a more traditional desktop experience. While GNOME Classic is based on GNOME 3 technologies, it provides several changes to the UI:

  - When your installation is completed, reboot your computer to start using your Ubuntu system with the GNOME desktop environment.

  - You can run the reboot command in the Terminal for a quick reboot.

Features:

- In Ubuntu version 19.10, the default Yaru theme introduced a dark version. Ubuntu 20.04 takes three variants of the default Yaru theme: Light, Dark, and Standard. You do not need to install GNOME Tweaks to switch between the default theme variants. This option is embedded into the Settings application. Ubuntu 20.04 also has a slightly different look, emphasizing the second accent color of aubergine.

- In GNOME 3.36, all the visual and performance improvements come with it. Ubuntu 20.04 has the latest GNOME 3.36 release. It means that all the new features in 3.36 are also available for Ubuntu 20.04.

- The one more thing is that now you do not need to scroll down to go to the lock screen anymore. With a single click and you'll be on the login screen.

- To toggle the desktop notifications, you can use the Do not disturb option.

- Linux Kernel 5.4 Ubuntu 20.04 features the latest LTS kernel, 5.4. It means that you get native ExFAT support and all the other performance improvements and new hardware supports that come with it.

- The new compression algorithms now take less time to install Ubuntu 20.04. Not only has that, but Ubuntu 20.04 also booted faster than 18.04.

- Ubuntu is not providing ISO files for 32-bit systems for a few years now. But at least existing 32-bit Ubuntu users could still upgrade to Ubuntu 18.04. That's not the case anymore. You cannot upgrade to Ubuntu 20.04 if you use 32-bit Ubuntu 18.04. If you try to run the upgrade, you'll see an error.

- The canonical company keeps on making its universal packaging format snap. It is even more apparent in Ubuntu 20.04 release. If you try to run a program that is not installed, it is used to suggest an apt command for installing it.

- But now, it suggests both snap and apt commands with snap command suggestions before apt.

Ubuntu and Debian Package Management Essentials
Introduction
The package is one of the fundamental advantages that Linux systems provide. The packaging format and the management tools vary to distribution, but two general families have emerged as the common.

For RHEL-based distros, the RPM packaging format and packaging tools like rpm and yum are standard. The other central family, used by

Debian, Ubuntu, and related distributions, uses the. deb packaging format and tools like apt and dpkg.

This section guide will cover some of the most common package management tools that system administrators use on Debian and Ubuntu systems. It can be a quick reference when you need to know how to perform a package management task within these systems.

Debian Package Management Tools Overview

The Debian-Ubuntu ecosystem is quite a few different package management tools to manage software on the system.

Most of these tools are work on the same package databases. Some of these tools provide high-level interfaces to the packaging system, while other utilities provide low-level functionality.

1. **Apt-get:** The apt-get command is probably the most used member of the apt suite of packaging tools. Its primary purpose is interfacing with remote repositories maintained by the distribution's packaging team and performing actions on the available packages.

   The apt suite generally removes information from the remote into a cache maintained on the local system. The apt-get is used to refresh the local cache. It is even used to modify the package state, meaning installing or removing a package from the system. In general, apt-get updates the local cache and modifies the live system.

2. **Apt-cache:** Another essential member of the apt suite is apt-cache and the utility uses the local cache to query the available packages and their properties.

   For instance, apt-cache is an excellent place to start when you wish to search for a specific package or a tool that will perform a particular function. It can also inform what procedure will target the exact package version. Dependency and reverse dependency is another area where apt-cache is useful.

3. **Aptitude:** The aptitude command combines the functionality of the above commands. It has the advantage as a command-line tool, combining the functionality of the two devices above, and can also work using a zNcurses text-based menued interface.

   When we operate from the command line, most of the commands mirror the abilities of apt-get and apt-cache exactly. Because of overlapping, we won't be examining aptitude extensively in this guide.

You can use aptitude in place of either apt-get or apt-cache if you prefer the tool.

- **Dpkg:** While the previous tools focused on managing packages maintained in repositories, the dpkg command can also operate on individual .deb packages. The dpkg tool is responsible for most of the behind-the-scenes work of the commands above.

    Unlike the apt-* commands, dpkg cannot resolve dependencies automatically. Its main feature is working with .deb packages directly and dissecting a package to learn more about its structure. Although it can gather information about the packages installed on your system, its purpose is on the individual package level.

- **Tasksel:** The tasksel program is a diff type of tool for managing software. Instead of managing single packages or even applications, tasksel focuses on grouping the software needed to accomplish specific "tasks." The organized tasks can select using a text-based interface.

- **Others:** Many other package management tools are available that provide separate functionality or present information in other ways. We only be touching on these as necessary, but they can be handy in certain situations. Some of the tools that fall into the category are apt-file, dselect, and gdebi.

- **Updating the Package Cache and the System:** The Debian-Ubuntu package managing tools provide a significant way to keep your system's list of available packages up-to-date. It also offers straightforward methods of updating packages you currently have installed on your server.

- **Updating the Package Cache and the System:** The Debian-Ubuntu package management tools provide a great way to keep the system's list of available packages up-to-date. It offers simple methods of updating packages installed on your server.

- **Update Local Package Cache:** The remote repositories that packaging tools rely on for package information are updated all of the time. However, the majority of the management tools work with a local-cache of this information.

    It is usually helpful to update your local package cache every session before executing other package commands. It ensures that you are operating on the most up-to-date information about the available software. Actually, to the point, some installation commands will fail if you work with stale package information.

To update the local cache, use the given command with the update sub-command:

```
$ sudo apt-get update
```

- **Update Packages without Package Removal:** The apt packaging suite makes to keep all of the software installed on your server up-to-date.

  The apt command varies between two different update procedures. First, the update procedure can upgrade any components that do not require component removal. See the selection below to learn how to update and allow apt to remove and swap parts as necessary.

  This can be very important when you do not want to remove any installed packages under any circumstance. However, some updates involve replacing system components or removing conflicting files. This procedure will ignore any updates that require package removal:

```
$ sudo apt-get upgrade
```

After performing this step, any update that does not involve removing components will be applied.

- **Update Packages and Remove As Necessary:** The apt packaging suite makes to keep all of the software installed on your server up-to-date.

  The apt command varies between two different update procedures. The first update procedure ignores any updates that require package removal.

  The second procedure will update all packages, even those that require package removal. It is often necessary as dependencies for packages change.

  Usually, the removed packages will be replaced by functional equivalents during the upgrade procedure, so this is generally safe. However, it is good to keep an eye on the packages to be removed, only in case some essential components are labeled for removal. To achieve this action, type:

```
$ sudo apt-get dist-upgrade
```

Downloading and Installing Packages

One of the main functions of package management tools is to facilitate downloading and installing packages onto the system.

- **Search for Packages:** When downloading and installing packages, the first step is to search your distribution's repositories for the packages you are looking for.

  Most apt commands operate primarily on the cache of package information maintained on the local machine, allowing quicker execution and less network traffic.

  Searching for packages is one operation that targets the package cache for information. The apt-cache search sub-command is the tool needed to search for available packages. Keep in mind that you should ensure that your local cache is up-to-date using sudo apt-get update before searching for packages:

```
$ apt-cache search package
```

- **Install a Package from the Repos:** We can use the apt-get command with the install sub-command to install a package from the repositories and all of the necessary dependencies.

  The parameters for this command should be the package name or names as they are labeled in the repository:

```
$ sudo apt-get install package
```

You can install multiple packages at once, separated by a space:

```
$ sudo apt-get install package1 package2
```

If your request package requires extra dependencies, these will be printed to standard out, and you will be asked to confirm the procedure. It will look something like this:

```
$ sudo apt-get install apache2
```

- **Install a Particular Package Version from the Repos:** If you need to install a specific version of a package, you can provide the version you would like to establish with an equal sign, like this:

```
$ sudo apt-get install package=version
```

The version, in this case, must match one of the package version numbers present in the repository. It means utilizing the versioning scheme employed by distribution. You can also find the available versions by typing the apt-cache policy package.

- **Reconfigure Packages:** Many packages include post-installation configuration scripts run after the installation is complete. These include prompts for the administrator to make configuration choices.

  If you need to execute these configuration steps later, you can use the dpkg-reconfigure command. The command looks at the package passed to it and re-runs any post-configuration commands included within the package specification:

  ```
  $ sudo dpkg-reconfigure package
  ```

- **Perform a Dry Run of Package Actions:** You will usually want to see the side effects of a procedure before without committing to executing the command. Fortunately, apt allows you to add the -s flag to "simulate" a procedure.

  For instance, to see what would be done if you choose to install a package, you can type:

  ```
  $ apt-get install -s package
  ```

  It will allow you to see all of the dependencies and the changes to the system that will take place if you remove the -s flag.

  By default, the apt will prompt the user to confirm many processes. It includes installations that require additional dependencies and package upgrades.

  To bypass these upgrades and default to accept any of these prompts, you can pass the -y flag when performing these operations:

  ```
  $ sudo apt-get install -y package
  ```

  It will install the package and any dependencies without further prompting from the user. It can be used for upgrade procedures as well:

  ```
  $ sudo apt-get dist-upgrade -y
  ```

You have searched for packages containing GNOME-desktop in all suites, sections, and architectures. Found 28 matching packages.

- Package bfh-GNOME-desktop
- Package GNOME-desktop-3-tests

- Package GNOME-desktop-3-tests-dbgsym

- Package GNOME-desktop-testing

- Package GNOME-desktop-testing-dbgsym

- Package GNOME-desktop3-data

- Package libGNOME-desktop-3-12

- Package libGNOME-desktop-3-17

- Package libGNOME-desktop-3-17-dbgsym

- Package libGNOME-desktop-3-19

Advantages:

- The solid OS for general uses purpose and newbies too.

- The cool orange-y custom theme looks quite refreshing than the original GNOME Adwaita theme.

- Ubuntu is a secured OS and defines the highest level of security compared to other OSs.

- Ubuntu is an open-source OS.

- Ubuntu is the popular Linux OS.

- Most of the software in Ubuntu are pre-installed to enhance user experience.

- It is available free of cost.

Disadvantages:

- The GNOME desktop is slightly modified, mimicking the old Ubuntu Unity desktop. So you cannot experience the (or vanilla) GNOME desktop its developers intended.

- Ubuntu is very conventional to new technologies. You can instead go for Fedora Distro.

- It is very wise to faults in hardware which makes it less steady than other OSs.

- There is little hardware support for Ubuntu OS. Some users complain that it becomes difficult to configure a modem to start work on the Internet.

- It is not possible to play modern games in Ubuntu OS. It shows poor graphics quality, and we have to use emulators to do, which harms the graphics quality.

FEDORA

The distro is recommended for computer geeks. It has a unique ecosystem that deploys new and updated software to its end users. While other major Linux distros like stability over new software feature updates, Fedora has a different philosophy. It has featured a vanilla GNOME desktop, and its developers as a development platform mean all the new feature-bit updates land on Fedora before any other Linux distros.

Fedora is a Linux's distribution developed by the community Fedora Project and owned by Red Hat. Fedora Linux contains software distributed under a free and open-source license and aims to be on the leading edge of such technologies. Fedora has a reputation for innovation, integrating new technologies, and working closely with upstream Linux communities. The default desktop in Fedora Linux is the GNOME desktop environment, and the default interface is the GNOME Shell. Other desktop environments are available, including KDE, Xfce, LXDE, MATE, and Cinnamon. Its project also distributes custom variations of Fedora called Fedora spins. These are built with specific software packages, offering alternative desktop environments or targeting specific interests such as gaming, security, design, scientific computing, and robotics.

Reasons to Use Fedora

1. **Fedora Is Bleeding Edge:** The Fedora OS is called a bleeding-edge Linux distribution because it is constantly rolling out with the latest software, driver updates, and Linux features. It contributes to why you can confidently use Fedora as soon as the installation is complete. It ships with the latest stable kernel with all its benefits.
For example, it is the first major distribution to use systemd as its default init system and the first distro to use Wayland as its default display server protocol.

2. **A Good Community:** Fedora has one of the significant communities globally, with a forum populated by many users who will happily help you sort out any issues that might have you stuck while using the distro.

3. **Fedora Spins:** Fedora is available in different flavors directed to the community as "spins," Each spin uses a different Desktop Environment from the default GNOME Desktop. The available Spins are KDE Plasma, XFCE, LXQT, Mate-Compiz, Cinnamon, LXDE, and SOAS.

4. **Prolific Hardware Support:** Fedora has many benefits gratitude to the communities backing it. A good example is readily Fedora will work on PCs, with printers, scanners, cameras, etc., from different vendors out of the box. If you want a Linux-based distro that wouldn't give you any compatibility headaches, then Fedora is a good choice.

5. **Fedora Is Easy to Use:** The Linux distros are well-known for their ease of use, and Fedora is among the easiest distributions to use. Its easy UI is simple enough for anyone to boot up for the first time and get used to after a couple of clicks. Its software offers the same user experience, which gives users a feeling of consistency and familiarity.

Benefits of Fedora

- **Enhanced Security Features:** The most vital feature in Fedora is Security. This open-source OS boasts Linux-based security, which incorporates several security policies. For example, Linux Kernel and Security modules allow mandatory access control.

- **Innovation:** Fedora is well-known for its new open-source software technologies. Its primary sponsor was responsible for several desktop enhancements, including HAL, Policy Kit, Ogg Theora, Network Manager, D-Bus, and AIGLX.

- **Reliability:** After using Fedora, all features work with ease as expected, with no problems whatsoever. While it provides updates to several packages, most users agree that it is still reliable.

- **Educational Software:** Fedora has an addition known as groups. Install the group you want such as KDE, Java, Perl, GNOME, or even Kernel.

- **Different Editions of Fedora Operating System:**

  - Fedora has released two new versions of OS per year, around May and November starting. After version 30, Fedora released different editions for different use cases.

  - Fedora Workstation is an edition for users who want a user-friendly OS for their laptops or desktop systems. As default, the GNOME desktop and also others can also be installed.

  - **Fedora Server:** The edition targets the servers, including those used in data center technologies. It does not have a pre-installed desktop but can be installed if needed. From version 28 and later, it supports alternative update streams.

  - **Fedora CoreOS:** The edition has the bare essentials of the OS, and it is focused on cloud computing, showing only the minimal image of the Fedora to give more space to develop.

  - **Fedora IoT:** As in the previous edition, in this edition, the features of the Fedora are minimized and optimized in a way that runs on the Internet of Things (IoT) devices.

  - **Fedora Silverblue:** The edition is the best choice for users who want immutable desktops, and the developers who use container-based workflows can also use it.

RPM-BASED

Red Hat Linux was the significant distribution that used the. rpm file format, which is used in several package management systems today. Both of these were divided into commercial and community-supported distributions. Red Hat Linux was split into a community-supported but Red Hat-sponsored distribution named Fedora and a commercially supported distribution called Red Hat Enterprise Linux. In contrast, SUSE was divided into openSUSE and SUSE Linux Enterprise.

GNOME-RPM

The GNOME Desktop provides another graphical RPM-management tool, GNOME-RPM. Also known as gnorpm, GNOME-RPM is very similar to KPackage in terms of its basic functionality, although GNOME-RPM can manage only RPMs.

ZORIN OS

Another Linux distro features GNOME desktop but more beautifully for Windows folks. Its latest version much looks like Windows 10. The OS comes pre-installed with WINE, software for running Windows programs. It allows Windows folks to feel genuinely at home with their new Linux OS.Zorin OS is Ubuntu-based and thus will need more time for deploying the latest GNOME desktop after each Ubuntu release.

Zorin OS is entirely graphical, with a graphical installer. For stability and security, it follows the long-term releases of the primary Ubuntu system. It uses its software repositories as well as Ubuntu's repositories. These repositories are accessible through the standard "apt-get" commands via the Linux terminal or a GUI-based software manager that provides an AppStore-like experience for users who don't wish to use the Terminal.

The OS also has several desktop layouts or themes to modify the desktop environment. The themes let users change the interface to resemble those of Microsoft Windows, macOS, or Ubuntu and allow the interface to be familiar regardless of the previous system a user has come from. As with all GNOME-based desktop environments, the look and feel of the desktop can be modified easily using GNOME extensions.

Advantages:

- Mimics Microsoft Windows interface. So a Windows user can smoothly migrate between the two OS without learning new quirky styles for operating each OS.

- The ultimate users get Zorin support, so if you are stuck on an issue, you can contact them, and they'll be glad to help.

Disadvantage:

- It is irrelevant for non-Windows users.

Install Zorin OS

A simple step guide to install Zorin OS alongside your existing OS or instead of it is as follows:

- To get Zorin OS16, visit their official site, https://zorin.com/os/download/. It has two editions: Pro and Core. The core and Lite is the free edition, whereas Pro is commercial.

- To create a Drive of Zorin OS, you need to flash the Zorin OS ".iso" file from your computer to a USB flash drive using an app called balenaEtcher.

- Insert the USB flash drive into your system.

- Double click on the balenaEtcher download file to run the app.

- If you download the ".zip" file, you need to right-click on the .zip file and select "Extract Here." Afterward, please open the newly-extracted folder and double-click on the balenaEtcher ".AppImage" file to run the app.

- Press "Flash from file" to select the downloaded Zorin OS ".iso" file on your computer. The file should generally be in your "Downloads" folder.

- Press "Select target" and choose the correct USB flash drive from the list.

- Press "Flash!" to begin writing Zorin OS to the USB flash drive.

- After a few minutes, the USB flash drive will be ready for booting into Zorin OS.

LINUX MINT CINNAMON

It is another Linux distro based on Ubuntu. It features a Cinnamon desktop originally forked from GNOME. Linux Mint looks the same as Windows as a start menu and taskbar panel at the bottom.The unique thing about Linux Mint Cinnamon is its software updater tool. It takes system stability further by categorizing software based on how it will affect the system. You can decide if you would like to use Linux Mint to take care of the updates for you or control which software gets updated and which doesn't.

Advantages:

- Best Linux distro when updating software by categories keeping stability in mind.

- It is recommended alternative for Windows geeks.

Disadvantages:

- Some GTK apps like Builder do not look even with the Cinnamon desktop.

- New users have no idea how to install the software or install the files they need to include for the programs they want and use.

- Some configuration changes have to be done as the Root User, and access to the main account is done indirectly through the Sudo command.

- Not knowing which distribution to use, even though the underlying OS is not that.

- People never use the help files it has, nor do they use the user documents it contains to answer questions they have.

- Commercial Software Vendors do not generally write their software for Linux use.

- Sometimes it could be buggy.

Installation on Linux Mint 12

Cinnamon is a free and open-source desktop environment for the X Window System that derives from GNOME 3 but follows traditional desktop metaphor conventions. Cinnamon is the primary desktop environment of the Linux Mint distribution and is available as an optional desktop for other Linux distributions and other Unix-like OSs.

Cinnamon was included in the Linux Mint 12 (Lisa) repository. If you have not done so, update your package list. To do so, open a terminal and enter:

```
$ sudo apt-get update
```

Afterward, you can install Cinnamon by entering:

```
$ sudo apt-get install Cinnamon
```

Cinnamon is downloaded and installed. Apply it after installation, log out of the current session and click on the wheel icon on the login screen to select Cinnamon.

Choose Cinnamon from the menu on the login screen. If you happen to find a login screen without the usual background picture, a simple Lightdm Manager tool can fix that for you quickly. To install, add the appropriate repository, update the package list, and install:

```
$ sudo apt-add-repository ppa:claudiocn/slm
$ sudo apt-get update
$ sudo apt-get install simple-lightdm-manager
```

Following attempts to extend GNOME 3 to suit the Linux Mint design goals, the Mint developers develop several GNOME 3 components to build an independent desktop environment. Desklets and Applets are no longer compatible with GNOME 3.

Cinnamon has received favorable coverage by the press, particularly for its ease of use and gentle learning curve. Concerning its conservative design model, Cinnamon is similar to the Xfce and GNOME 2 desktop environments.

Software Components
X-Apps

Cinnamon introduces X-Apps based on GNOME Core Applications but is changed to work across Cinnamon, MATE, and XFCE; they have the traditional UI.

- **Xed:** It is a text editor based on Gedit/pluma.

- **Xviewer:** It is an image viewer based on Eye of GNOME.

- **Xreader:** It is a document viewer based on Evince/Atril.

- **Xplayer:** It is a media player based on GNOME Videos (Totem).

- **Pix:** It is an image organizer based on gThumb.

Features

Some features provided by Cinnamon include:

- The desktop effects, animations, transition effects, and transparency using composition;

- Panels equipped with a main menu, launchers, a window list and the system tray can be adjusted on the left, right, the upper or lower edge of the screen;

- Various extensions;

- There is applets that appear on the panel;

- The overview with functions similar to that in GNOME Shell; and

- Settings editor for easy customization. It can customize:

  - The panel

- The calendar

- Themes

- Desktop effects

- Applets

- Extensions

- Volume and brightness adjustment using scroll wheel while pointing at the respective taskbar icon.

As of January 24, 2012, there was no documentation for Cinnamon itself, although most documentation for GNOME Shell applies to Cinnamon. There is documentation for the Cinnamon edition of Linux Mint, with a chapter on the Cinnamon desktop.

DEBIAN TESTING

The first Linux Distro with GNOME desktop in our list is Debian Testing. This Linux distribution appears with the GNOME desktop by default. It will not be permanent, but it will be changed after some years due to technological evolution over time.

Debian has many features of the real GNOME Desktop, but it doesn't contain some new software available in other Distros.

The good thing about Debian is that it helps you to report bugs directly to the community and provides you with suggestions through which you can accomplish all of your computing needs.

Advantages:

- It gives you the experience of a vanilla GNOME desktop.

- Debian is known for being highly stable and continuously patched.

Disadvantages:

- This OS requires more knowledge about its maintenance because there are many chances that you will face misbehaving software.

- You have to exist with different software bugs because of its testing version.

GNOME in Debian

GNOME is one of the desktop environment options in the Debian desktop.

Versions

- DebianBullseye includes GNOME 3.38.

- DebianBuster includes GNOME 3.30.

- DebianStretch includes GNOME 3.22.

- DebianJessie includes GNOME 3.14.

- DebianWheezy includes GNOME 3.4.

- DebianSqueeze includes GNOME 2.30.

For the development distributions DebianUnstable-DebianTesting, you can refer to the versions of the individual packages such as GNOME-shell. During the transitions between versions, the GNOME packages are not necessarily all at the same version.

Options

There are three methods to install GNOME in Debian, as discussed in the following table.

GNOME Desktop Task	Description
GNOME (Debian)	Debian's selection of applications
	It includes some applications that do not really integrate with GNOME, like LibreOffice and Firefox
GNOME (Debian)	The full GNOME environment, including applications that are not officially part of the Upstream GNOME releases
	It provides the recommended GNOME environment for Debian
GNOME (core only)	Only the official "core" modules of the GNOME desktop. Above packages depend on this one

For developers:

- **GNOME-core-devel:** The development packages to compile GNOME dependent packages from source.

- **GNOME-devel:** A full development suite for developing GNOME-based applications.

- **GNOME-api-docs:** The complete API documentation for all GNOME libraries.

Installing "GNOME Desktop" Task

The GNOME Desktop task is what is installed by Debian-Installer's Desktop "task".

You can install it manually using apt:

```
$ apt-get install task-gnome-desktop
```

ELEMENTARY OS

It is a Linux-based on Ubuntu LTS. It promotes a "thoughtful, capable, and ethical" replacement to macOS and Windows and has a pay-what-you-want model. The desktop environment called Pantheon and accompanying applications are developed and maintained by Elementary, Inc.

The guidelines of the elementary OS project focus on usability with a gentle learning curve rather than full-fledged customization. The three core rules the developers set were "concision," "accessible configuration," and "minimal documentation."

Elementary OS has to get praise and criticism for its design.

It is closely resembled macOS, visually and in user experience. The elementary developers maintain that any similarities are unintentional.

Pantheon's main shell is integrated with other elementary OS applications, like Plank (i.e., a dock), Web (a default web browser based on Epiphany), and Code (a simple text editor). This distribution uses Gala as its window manager, based on Mutter.

We have many familiar desktop environments with Windows-like GNOME desktop, but we also have an option about GNOME Linux distro that looks like Apple desktop. Elementary OS have a desktop named Pantheon. It's still GNOME tweaked to make look like it as Apple.

Such as Zorin OS, Elementary is also based on Ubuntu. Hence, it features specific apps that integrate with the Pantheon desktop. For instance, the Epiphany web browser looks more straightforward and Apple-like than the Firefox web browser.

Moreover, the Linux distro features its own AppCenter, where you can find both free and pay-what-you-want software.

Advantages:

- There is the ease of migration to Linux for long-time users of Apple computers.

- It focused on privacy.

Disadvantage:

- Irrelevant for non-Apple users.

Elementary OS 6 is a significant upgrade after a few good years of updates to the 5.x series.

While the 5.x series has numerous feature updates and improvements, elementary OS 6 looks like an exciting endeavor.

Here, we shall look at all the new features and additions that have been presented with elementary OS 6.

1. **Dark Style and Accent Color:** Elementary OS has the dark style theme similar to how mainstream options work, opt-in preference. You can choose it from the login screen right after installing elementary OS 6.

   While adding a dark mode may sound like something minor, they seem to have put a great deal of effort into providing a consistent dark mode overall. All the first-party applications support both the dark style and light theme. Elementary OS will let the app developers and users' preference in elementary OS 6. And if the user prefers a dark mode or light mode, the app can adapt to that.

2. **Improved Notifications and Redesigned Notification Center:** The notifications can support icon badges and action buttons, making up for a better experience. It could let you quickly open links, mark a message read, along with several other possibilities, and urgent notifications have a new look and a unique sound to help you identify them. In addition to the notification, the notification center has also been redesigned to look better and clean with multiple notifications.

3. **First-Party Flatpak Apps and Permissions View:** Chose the Flatpak-first approach to improve privacy and security across the platform in elementary OS 6. Elementary OS has its AppCenter Flatpak repository.

The default applications come in as Flatpak packages, and all the applications listed in AppCenter are available as Flatpaks. Overall means a better sandboxing experience where all applications stay isolated from each other without accessing sensitive data. Elementary OS 6 adds the "Portals," The applications request permission to access files or launch another application. You can also get to control all the permissions from the System Settings.

4. **Multi-Touch Gestures:** The new multi-touch gestures are handy for Laptop and touchpad users, you can do it all using multi-touch gestures, from accessing the multitasking view to navigating the workspaces. Not just limited to certain functions on the desktop, you can also interact with notifications, swipe via applications, and have a seamless system experience with the new multi-touch gestures. You can also customize the gestures or learn more about them from the Gestures section under the System Settings.

5. **Improved Desktop Workflow and Screenshot Utility:** The multitasking view lets you differentiate among multiple active windows. And the corners view lets move the window to a new workspace and maximizes the window as well. The screenshot utility can be moved around in the window, not just stuck to the center of the window. You can drag-drop the image from the preview without saving it.

Pantheon Desktop Environment

The Pantheon desktop is built on top of the GNOME software, i.e., GTK, GDK, Cairo, GLib, GObject and GIO, GVfs, and Tracker. The desktop allows for multiple workspaces to organize the user's workflow.

Pantheons applications are designed and developed by elementary include:

- **Pantheon Greeter:** It is a session manager based on LightDM.

- **Gala:** It is a window manager.

- **Wingpanel:** It is a top panel, similar in function to GNOME Shell's top panel.

- **Slingshot:** It is an application launcher located in WingPanel.

- **Plank:** It is a dock on which Docky is based.

- **Switchboard:** Settings application (or control panel).

- **Pantheon Mail:** E-mail client is written in Vala and based on WebKitGTK.

- **Calendar:** Desktop calendar.

- **Music:** Audio player.

- **Code:** code-focused text editor, comparable to gedit or leafpad.

- **Terminal:** Terminal emulator.

- **Files:** It is a file manager formerly called Marlin.

- **Installer:** Installer built in partnership with System76.

- Bryan Lunduke of Network World wrote that the Pantheon desktop environment, elementary OS's centerpiece, was among the best environments of 2016.

- Pantheon is also an optional desktop environment in GeckoLinux.

Some other notable changes include:

- The camera app has a new UI for switching cameras, mirror images, and more.

- AppCenter does not list Flatpak apps can now notify you when an application has completed installation to open it quickly.

- The files app has also received improvements in a new sidebar and list view. Also, a double-click is required to open a file, and a single click can navigate via folders.

ARCH LINUX

Arch Linux is the distribution of choice for many hobbyists that users can build themselves. The central focus of the OS is to provide the latest software as soon as it's available, as fast as possible.

Due to the quick updates that Arch Linux users have access to, they can quickly get the latest and greatest GNOME Shell and GNOME-related features, much like on Fedora. Best of all, since Arch Linux is "build it yourself," you won't find any customizations or unwanted extensions!

To use Arch Linux, you will need to head over to ArchLinux.org. Once you've completed it to the website, locate the "Download" button at the top to go to the download page. There are various methods for downloading the latest ISO release of the OS on the Arch Linux download page.

Install GNOME Desktop Environment In Arch Linux

Firstly, check that you have updated your Arch Linux system.

```
$ sudo pacman -Syu
```

After updating, reboot the system to apply the latest updates.

```
$ sudo reboot
```

Next, Install X Window System (xorg) using the command:

```
$ sudo pacman -S xorg xorg-server
```

Finally, install GNOME Desktop environment using the command as follow:

```
$ sudo pacman -S gnome
```

The command will install all needed applications including the GNOME display manager for the GNOME desktop environment.

How to start and enable gdm service:

```
$ sudo systemctl start gdm.service
$ sudo systemctl enable gdm.service
```

You can use other popular DMs. Here are the popular graphical DMs used by Linux OSs.

- **LightDM:** It is a cross-desktop display manager that can use various front-ends written in any toolkit.

- **LXDM:** The LXDE display manager can be used independently of the LXDE desktop environment.

- **MDM:** MDM display manager is used in Linux Mint, a fork of GDM 2.

- **SDDM:** It is a QML-based display manager and successor to KDE4's kdm; recommended for Plasma 5 and LXQt.

- **XDM:** It is X display manager with support for XDMCP, host chooser.

OPENSUSE

openSUSE also gives you access to vanilla GNOME. But unlike Fedora, it follows a much slower release schedule. You won't get access to all the latest GNOME features as soon as they are released. However, this isn't technically a bad thing.

openSUSE can dedicate more time and effort to make the OS more stable and reliable by having a slow release cycle. It makes it a perfect fit for professionals who can't afford to have their system crash in the middle of meaningful work.

Now, openSUSE is distributed under two release models – Leap and Tumbleweed.

Each major version is released every three years, whereas point releases or minor updates are released annually with Leap. We have Tumbleweed, with a rolling release edition. It does not require any significant upgrades apart from minor updates and snapshots from time to time.

Depending on how often you want to upgrade your system, you should pick the flavor.

Installing GNOME

GNOME implements the classic "desktop" elegantly because of its vast popularity – all the major Linux distros, including openSUSE, support GNOME. We will be using YaST as it is the easiest way to manage desktop environments.

Search for YaST in the menu and enter the root password.

Select "Software Management."

Select "Pattern" from the "View" drop-down menu

All environments are placed under the section of "Graphical Environments." Then right-click on "GNOME Desktop Environment (X11)" and select "Install." We're going with the x-server version because the x server has been around for years. It is compatible with most of the programs.

This step is optional. You can also choose to uninstall the previous desktop environment. In my case, it's KDE Plasma and its related apps.

When you're ready, click "Accept."

The list will give you a summary of what changes are being made. Click "Continue."

It takes time to download and install/uninstall the necessary packages. Have a cup of coffee in the meantime!

Once the installation is complete, it'll show a short report of the installation process. Click "Finish."

Reboot your computer.

From the bottom-left corner, select "GNOME" from the drop-down menu.

SOLUS

Solus, also known as Evolve OS, is a developed OS for the x86 64 architecture based on the Linux kernel and the homegrown Budgie desktop environment, GNOME, MATE, or KDE Plasma desktop environment. Its package manager is based on the PiSi package management system from Pardus Linux. It has a semi-rolling release model, with new package updates landing in the stable repository every Friday. The developers of Solus have stated that Solus is intended exclusively for use on personal computers and will not include software that is only useful in enterprise or server environments.

Solus 1.0 "Shannon" was released on December 27, 2015. Solus 1.1 was released on February 2, 2016. HecticGeek blogger Gayan has described Solus 1.1 as a "well optimized operating system," praising significantly faster boot and shutdown times than Ubuntu 15.10. Due to several usability issues encountered, he recommended waiting another year before trying it out again.

Solus 1.2 was launched on June 20, 2016. Solus 1.2.0.5 was on September 7, 2016. Solus 1.2.1 was on October 19, 2016. It is the last fixed point release of Solus, and all future releases will be based on the snapshot model.

Editions

Solus is currently available in four editions:

- Budgie flagship edition has a "feature-rich, luxurious desktop using the most modern technologies."

- GNOME running the GNOME desktop environment, "a contemporary desktop experience."

- MATE edition uses the MATE desktop environment, a "traditional desktop for advanced users and older hardware."

- KDE Plasma edition is a "a sophisticated desktop experience for the tinkerers."

Solus is an attractive GNOME-based Linux distribution and comparatively new to other distros. It is built from scratch. By default, it comes with a new and custom desktop environment called "Budgie". But it has a GNOME-supported version also. What is unique about this distribution is that it offers several features. The key feature is a lightweight, highly customizable, platform-independent, and feature-rich OS.

However, this OS is straightforward to use. Therefore, go for Solus if you are a beginner and want to try out a basic system. It could be a good option before moving on to more complex setups.

MANJARO GNOME EDITION

Manjaro Linux, known merely as Manjaro, is an "open-source OS for computers. The OS is a circulation of Linux based on Arch Linux's distribution and emphasizes the users' approachability and accessibility.

It aims to work entirely out of the box because of its variation of the pre-installed program. Moreover, it includes an updated rolling release model and utilizes "Pacman" as package administrator. In other words, this is simply an amazing OS that we recommend you to use blindly.

Reasons to Use Manjaro

The reasons why many computer users choose Manjaro Linux are followed here, with a detailed clarification of each.

- **Effortless to Install:** The installation of Manjaro is straightforward, taking only 20 minutes, and the entire process is more remarkable than that of Windows. To install it, you need to download Manjaro, then use Etcher to burn it to a USB and boot inside the USB drive. After that, run the installer and select your country, keyboard language, where to install.

- **Supportive Hardware:** When you install Linux, you may find it problematic to have each hardware functioning. But, if Manjaro Linux is installed, you don't have to face such an issue. This OS tests the system at first and then installs the mandatory drivers.

- **Availability of Software:** Considering that the "Manjaro" team holds a huge software storehouse would be best. Similarly, the users of Manjaro have an easy entry to the "Arch User Repository."

- **Easy Switching to Kernels:** It would be best to use some terminal wizardry to switch to kernels on the maximum number of distros, whereas Manjaro owns an excellent tiny program that lets you install kernels as many as you require.

- **Time-Saving:** The Arch is a rolling release, and the users often face a significant problem that a fresh bundle will be unrestricted that may break the system. The team works hard to evade that issue by examining new packages before making these available for the users. It may make Manjaro considerably less than the bleeding edge; this also confirms that new packages will be much quicker than distros with planned releases like Ubuntu. It is thought that Manjaro is a decent selection to be a productive machine.

- **Privacy and Security:** Manjaro is from many other OS from numerous perspectives. Its privacy offering method is also admirable. The security of this OS is so sufficient that you won't need to worry about devices being hacked by any stranger.
  Moreover, the OS is designed perfectly for destroying the harmful malware that is often responsible for the loss of your valuable data. It is how Manjaro safeguards your privacy from years to years.

- **The Ultimate Use of GUI:** GUI is, known as "Graphical User Interfaces," is used by Manjaro in the best way to ensure that the installers can have both an enjoyable and helpful interface.

- **No More Hassle with PPAs:** When you use any Linux Mint or Lubuntu, you will deal with heaps of PPAs. It refers to a repo only for a single task or a trivial set of programs. Installation of any software unavailable in the authorized Ubuntu Repos requires connecting a new PPA to your system through the Terminal.

The application is available for installation only when the new PPA is connected, and you operate the update of "sudo apt-get." Manjaro Linux doesn't use Ubuntu as its base; instead, it uses Arch that doesn't require PPAs.

CHAPTER SUMMARY

So these were some of the top GNOME-based Linux distros. As you can see, there is a whole variety of distros specializing in different things, so you can pick the one that resonates with your needs and requirements. For example, go with Fedora or Arch if you are looking for vanilla GNOME with access to all the latest features as soon as they are released.

On the other hand, if you look for a little more stability, then Debian, openSUSE, and Mageia are excellent alternatives, with CentOS being the most stable and reliable with a long-term release cycle. However, suppose you want to stay in the middle and access new features in a reasonably timely fashion without sacrificing stability. In that case, you can try out Manjaro or POP!_OS, both of which are incredibly beginner-friendly.

And finally, if you want to use GNOME because of its features and are not concerned about how it looks, go with Ubuntu or Zorin OS. Both provide you with a heavily customized GNOME desktop, but they are filled with valuable features and welcome new users.

Appraisal

Since its early years, the Ubuntu operating system has taken the open-source and the IT world by storm. From the Little Operating System That Could, it has grown into a fully-featured desktop and server offering that has won users' hearts everywhere. Besides the strong technical platform and impressive dedication to quality, Ubuntu also enjoys success because of its vast community of enthusiastic users who help support, document, and test every point of the Ubuntu landscape.

In your hands, you have the official, qualified guide to this unique operating system. Each of us working on this book has shown a high level of technical competence and willingness to share this knowledge. We gathered together to create a book that offers a solid understanding of Ubuntu and explains how the many fundamentals and features of the Ubuntu GNOME desktop environment work.

The GNOME desktop environment has become the most popular, arguably, and one of the best-loved popular Linux distributions. Its name translates to humanity toward others. Its focus on support for many languages and special needs has reflected the ideals of spreading free software over the standard Linux target markets: corporate servers.

Many popular Linux distros use GNOME as their default desktop environment, and it has some popular forks, such as Linux Mint Cinnamon.

GNOME was created to be easy to use and customizable. Its user interface aims to provide a unique experience.

Unfortunately, GNOME is not a lightweight desktop environment. So, it's not good to choose to work with if you want to install a Linux distribution on older computers or systems with less than 4 gigs of RAM.

But it is good to see that GNOME is focusing on the performance side of things with their latest GNOME 3.36 release. So, if you want to use a good user experience that looks different from a traditional Windows layout,

DOI: 10.1201/9781003311942-6

GNOME should be the perfect pick. GNOME's major distros are Ubuntu, Debian, Fedora, openSUSE. Pop OS 20.04 also features many good things, and a GNOME desktop environment.

This book can vary in coverage from deep over various topics. It is intentional. Any other book does not cover some topics, and they deserve deep coverage here. There are some topics that power users master. Other topics are things the power users should know about. They can understand some history, some other options, or have what they need to listen to further discussions with different technical views without being completely confused.

This book is planned for intermediate and advanced users or those who want to become middle and advanced users. Our goal is to give you the right direction, to help you enter the higher stages by guiding you to use as many tools and ideas as possible. We give you some thoughts and methods to consider that you can seek out more. Although the contents are for intermediate to advanced users, new users who pay attention will benefit from each chapter where all chapters are related to one another. The central pointer is that more detailed or related information is provided at the end of each chapter.

This book helps you to learn these skills and tells you how to learn more about your system, Linux, including Ubuntu Distros with the desktop environment. Most importantly, it enables you to overcome your fear of the system by telling you more about it and how it works. You can also install the other Linux distros like Fedora, openSUSE, elementary OS, Manjaro, etc.

This book is more than just a pure reference book and properly guides you with step-by-step procedures for performing tasks. The book is organized by topics and includes as many useful commands as possible.

Chapter 1 contains the basic understanding of the Ubuntu system with GNOME installation and how it is different from other Linux distro systems and some specific terms like GUI, CLI, and TUI. It describes the vast resources available to support this book. You will get brief knowledge of GNOME history, features, and some pros and cons as well.

Chapter 2 provides a quick review of the GNOME installation in UBUNTU, describes useful commands such as apt-get snapd, and gives you brief knowledge of the user interface of the GNOME environment system.

Chapter 3 provides a quick review of the installation of GNOME-based applications like Corebird, FeedReader, Snappy, EasyTag, and also describes their features of various components with the user interface.

Chapter 4 provides a quick review of the topic GTK, its history, GIMP (GIMP Drawing Kit), Software Architecture, various binding languages of GTK, and desktop environments based on GTK. This chapter also covers GTK+ with the creation of a simple GTK program.

Chapter 5 provides you with knowledge of the other GNOME-based Linux Distros like Ubuntu and DEB Family, Fedora, Zorin OS, Linux Mint Cinnamon, openSUSE, Solus, etc.

In other words, the book is meant to help you as you work on an Ubuntu distro with a GNOME desktop environment or another operating system.

Bibliography

About Manjaro – Manjaro. (2022, March 27). Manjaro; wiki.manjaro.org. https://wiki.manjaro.org/index.php/About_Manjaro

Apps – GNOME Wiki! (n.d.). Apps – GNOME Wiki!; wiki.gnome.org. Retrieved July 11, 2022, from https://wiki.gnome.org/Apps

Beal, V. (2001, January 4). *What is GNU Network Object Model Environment (GNOME)?* Webopedia; www.webopedia.com. https://www.webopedia.com/definitions/gnome/

Bodnar, J. (2022, January 6). *Introduction to GTK+.* Introduction to GTK+; zetcode.com. https://zetcode.com/gui/gtk2/introduction/

Chapter 1. Introducing the GNOME 3 Desktop Red Hat Enterprise Linux 7 | Red Hat Customer Portal. (n.d.). Red Hat Customer Portal; access.redhat.com. Retrieved July 11, 2022, from https://access.redhat.com/documentation/enus/red_hat_enterprise_linux/7/html/desktop_migration_and_administration_guide/introducing-gnome3-desktop

Current GTK+ development. (n.d.). GTK+ History; people.redhat.com. Retrieved July 11, 2022, from https://people.redhat.com/mclasen/Usenix04/notes/x29.html#:~:text=GTK%2B%20was%20started%20as%20toolkit,needed%20to%20support%20the%20GIMP

Das, A. (2021, August 24). *The Best Desktop Environments For Linux (We Tested Them So That You Don't Have To).* It's FOSS; itsfoss.com. https://itsfoss.com/best-linux-desktop-environments/

DesktopEnvironment – Debian Wiki. (n.d.). DesktopEnvironment – Debian Wiki; wiki.debian.org. Retrieved July 11, 2022, from https://wiki.debian.org/DesktopEnvironment

GDK – Wikipedia. (n.d.). GDK – Wikipedia; en.wikipedia.org. Retrieved July 11, 2022, from https://en.wikipedia.org/wiki/GDK

Getting GNOME – GNOME. (n.d.). Getting GNOME – GNOME; www.gnome.org. Retrieved July 11, 2022, from https://www.gnome.org/getting-gnome/

Getting Started with the GNOME Desktop | GNOME User Guide | openSUSE Leap 42.2. (n.d.). Getting Started with the GNOME Desktop | GNOME User Guide | openSUSE Leap 42.2; doc.opensuse.org. Retrieved July 11, 2022, from https://doc.opensuse.org/documentation/leap/archive/42.2/gnomeuser/html/book.gnomeuser/cha.gnomeuser.start.html

GNOME – ArchWiki. (n.d.). GNOME – ArchWiki; wiki.archlinux.org. Retrieved July 11, 2022, from https://wiki.archlinux.org/title/GNOME

GNOME – Wikipedia. (1999, March 3). GNOME – Wikipedia; en.wikipedia.org. https://en.wikipedia.org/wiki/GNOME

GNOME Programming in Linux using GTK+ LG #70. (n.d.). GNOME Programming in Linux Using GTK+ LG #70; linuxgazette.net. Retrieved July 11, 2022, from https://linuxgazette.net/issue70/ghosh2.html

GTK – Wikipedia. (1998, April 14). GTK – Wikipedia; en.wikipedia.org. https://en.wikipedia.org/wiki/GTK#:~:text=Gtk%23%20is%20a%20set%20of,Common%20Language%20Runtime%20(CLR)

Gtk.Builder. (n.d.). Gtk.Builder; docs.gtk.org. Retrieved July 11, 2022, from https://docs.gtk.org/gtk3/class.Builder.html#:~:text=A%20GtkBuilder%20is%20an%20auxiliary,gtk_builder_new_from_resource()%20or%20gtk_builder_new_from_string()

Gtk-3.0. (n.d.). Gtk – 3.0; docs.gtk.org. Retrieved July 11, 2022, from https://docs.gtk.org/gtk3/

How to Install a Desktop (GUI) on an Ubuntu Server. (2019, May 16). Knowledge Base by phoenixNAP; phoenixnap.com. https://phoenixnap.com/kb/how-to-install-a-gui-on-ubuntu

How to install and use gThumb on Ubuntu. (n.d.). How to Install and Use gThumb on Ubuntu; linuxhint.com. Retrieved July 11, 2022, from https://linuxhint.com/install-gthumb-ubuntu/

How to install and use Joplin note-taking app on Ubuntu 20.04. (n.d.). How to Install and Use Joplin Note-Taking App on Ubuntu 20.04; linuxhint.com. Retrieved July 11, 2022, from https://linuxhint.com/install_joplin_note_taking_app_ubuntu/

Introduction to the GNOME desktop – Linux – Lenovo Support IN. (n.d.). Introduction to the GNOME Desktop – Linux – Lenovo Support IN; support.lenovo.com. Retrieved July 11, 2022, from https://support.lenovo.com/in/en/solutions/ht510815-introduction-to-the-gnome-desktop-linux

Part I. GTK+ Overview: GTK+ 3 Reference Manual. (n.d.). Part I. GTK+ Overview: GTK+ 3 Reference Manual; www.manpagez.com. Retrieved July 11, 2022, from https://www.manpagez.com/html/gtk3/gtk3-3.16.3/gtk.php

Rahul. (2018, April 22). *How to Install Corebird Twitter Client on Ubuntu 18.04 & 16.04 LTS.* TecAdmin; tecadmin.net. https://tecadmin.net/install-corebird-twitter-client-on-ubuntu/

Reynolds, L. (2022, May 17). *Linux Tutorials – Learn Linux Configuration.* How to Install Gnome on Ubuntu 20.04 LTS Focal Fossa. https://linuxconfig.org/how-to-install-gnome-on-ubuntu-20-04-lts-focal-fossa

Rhythmbox Music Player – GNOME Library. (n.d.). Rhythmbox Music Player – GNOME Library; help.gnome.org. Retrieved July 11, 2022, from https://help.gnome.org/users/rhythmbox/

Simple Ways to Install Gnome on Ubuntu: 8 Steps (with Pictures). (2021, July 27). wikiHow; www.wikihow.com. https://www.wikihow.com/Install-Gnome-on-Ubuntu

Sneddon, J. (2020, February 18). *GNOME 3.36: The 10 Best New Features – OMG! Ubuntu!* OMG! Ubuntu!; www.omgubuntu.co.uk. https://www.omgubuntu.co.uk/2020/02/gnome-3-36-features

Sohail. (2019, April 7). *Best GNOME Desktops For 2022*. LinuxAndUbuntu; www. linuxandubuntu.com. https://www.linuxandubuntu.com/home/gnome-desktops

The 10 Best GNOME based Linux Distributions in 2020 | FOSS Linux. (2020, September 23). FOSS Linux; www.fosslinux.com. https://www.fosslinux. com/43280/the-10-best-gnome-based-linux-distributions.htm

Ubuntu and Debian Package Management Essentials | DigitalOcean. (2014, November 3). Ubuntu and Debian Package Management Essentials | DigitalOcean; www.digitalocean.com. https://www.digitalocean.com/ community/tutorials/ubuntu-and-debian-package-management-essentials

Ubuntu GNOME – javatpoint. (n.d.). Www.Javatpoint.Com; www.javatpoint.com. Retrieved July 11, 2022, from https://www.javatpoint.com/ubuntu-gnome

Visual overview of GNOME. (n.d.). Visual Overview of GNOME; help.gnome.org. Retrieved July 11, 2022, from https://help.gnome.org/users/gnome-help/sta-ble/shell-introduction.html.en

webmaster@debian.org, D. W. (n.d.). *Debian -- Package Search Results -- gnome-desktop*. Debian -- Package Search Results -- Gnome-Desktop; packages. debian.org. Retrieved July 11, 2022, from https://packages.debian.org/ search?keywords=gnome-desktop

What Is GNOME? (2021, June 1). SearchDataCenter; www.techtarget.com. https://www.techtarget.com/searchdatacenter/definition/GNOME-GNU-Network-Object-Model-Environment

Index